Fashion Exposed

| Graphics, promotion and advertising | Promotion, publicité et mode
| Promoción, publicidad y moda | Propaganda, publicidade e moda

promopress

Fashion Exposed

Graphics, promotion and advertising
Promotion, publicité et mode
Promoción, publicidad y moda
Propaganda, publicidade e moda

English preface revised by: Tom Corkett
Translators of the preface: French / Spanish / Brazilian Portuguese translator:
Marie-Pierre Teuler / Jesús de Cos Pinto / Élcio Carillo

PROMOPRESS is a commercial brand of:
Promotora de Prensa Internacional S.A.
C/ Ausiàs March, 124
08013 Barcelona, Spain
Phone: +34 93 245 14 64
Fax: +34 93 265 48 83
info@promopress.es
www.promopress.es
www.promopresseditions.com

Sponsored by Design 360°
– Concept and Design Magazine

Edited and produced by
Sandu Publishing Co., Ltd.
Book design, concepts & art direction by
Sandu Publishing Co., Ltd.
sandu.publishing@gmail.com

Cover Images by Emma Wickström

ISBN 978-84-92810-77-2

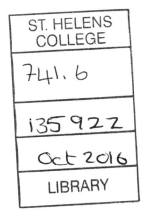
Printed in China

Expressing Self-Expression
Johanna Bonnevier

More than anything else, the fashion industry is about self-expression. Designing graphics in the world of fashion amounts in many respects to an act of conveying the idea of self-expression, making it an extension of fashion—a brief glimpse of what you could become—itself.

The focus of fashion advertising and graphics is often on just that, on 'what you could become.' Fashion is about moving forwards, to new trends and to the next 'thing,' and designing graphics for this requires a careful balancing act between what the customer is and what they want to be.

This is of course easier said than done—even if there are numerous ways of achieving it—but one thing most fashion-industry graphics design has in common is its attention to detail, something that is needed to stand out within a stream of constant information. Materials, typography, illustration and a range of other qualities are all important in the creation of that perfect communication between the brand and its customer. More often than in any other industry we see groundbreaking usage of printed materials and graphic techniques. As the quality, material and design of the clothing evolve, so do the graphics.

Fashion films, a medium which ever-more advanced technology and increasing amounts of time and money are used to produce, have become increasingly popular. Designing graphics for this relatively young genre presents new challenges and opens up further modes of expression for the designer.

Additionally, luxury brands are raising the bar each year during fashion shows around the world with both their show spaces and all their related accompaniments, such as invites—these things are a particularly potent way for a brand to create that ever-important first impression. It is this attention to detail along with coherent communication across all aspects of design that makes the difference that allows a brand to be noticed within that constant stream of information that fights for the customer's attention.

During the last decade digital media has become an increasingly important feature for any brand as it tries to engage in a conversation with its customers. The phrase 'lifestyle' has passed into almost all industries, and into fashion more than any others. Many are the fashion brands that are exploring a broad range of media, such as magazines, films and social media, all in the search for a more comprehensive 'lifestyle' approach that makes them stand out.

Creating such an extraordinary work is most often a collaboration between many talented creatives. Designers, art directors, copywriters and photographers amongst others are all an important part in the creative process, and it's the combined vision from these disciplines that creates powerful graphics.

Johanna Bonnevier
Johanna Bonnevier is a Swedish art director, graphic designer and illustrator based in East London. She mainly works on projects based around architecture, culture and fashion, ranging from both small- and large-scale print jobs to film credits and installations.

Expressing Self-Expression
Johanna Bonnevier

La mode est la seule industrie qui s'intéresse avant tout à l'expression de la personnalité et à l'affirmation de soi. Le travail d'un graphiste de mode consiste essentiellement à transmettre l'image que vous souhaitez projeter.

La publicité et le graphisme de mode sont axés presque exclusivement sur cette autre expression de nous-même. La mode n'est pas un univers statique aux canons immuables : c'est une force qui avance inexorablement vers la prochaine tendance et la dernière nouveauté. Le graphiste de mode doit constamment jongler entre ce que les clients sont vraiment et ce qu'ils voudraient être.

La mission du graphiste est donc particulièrement délicate, même s'il a accès à de multiples ressources pour l'aider dans sa tâche. L'industrie et le dessin de mode ont en commun l'attention au détail, la recherche de ce petit quelque chose qui fera toute la différence dans le flot d'informations diffusées à jet continu. Le choix des supports, de la typographie, des illustrations et un certain nombre de qualités permettront d'assurer la correspondance parfaite entre la marque et le client. L'industrie de la mode est pratiquement toujours la première à adopter des types de supports et des techniques graphiques révolutionnaires. Ainsi, le graphiste de mode doit s'adapter à mesure que la qualité, les matières et les styles évoluent.

Actuellement, la production de vidéos de mode, qui tire parti des progrès technologiques, a le vent en poupe. De plus en plus de gens sont prêts à y investir du temps et de l'argent.

Ce support relativement nouveau pour le graphisme de mode lance de nombreux défis et ouvre des possibilités d'expression inédites.

Chaque année, les marques de luxe mettent la barre encore un peu plus haut. Au cours des défilés de mode organisés dans le monde entier, elles conçoivent des espaces et des activités périphériques, dont certaines sur invitation, qui mettent magnifiquement en scène leurs nouveaux produits de façon à conquérir le public. C'est cette attention apportée aux détails couplée à une politique de communication cohérente touchant tous les aspects du design qui distingueront une marque des milliers d'autres qui tentent sans relâche de capter l'attention des gens.

Depuis dix ans, les marques se reposent de plus en plus sur les médias numériques pour rester en contact permanent avec leurs clients. De toutes les industries, c'est celle de la mode qui exploite le plus large éventail de supports de communication, allant du magazine à la vidéo, en passant par les médias sociaux : tout ce qui lui permet de sortir du lot l'intéresse.

Et tout ce fabuleux travail qui consiste à faire connaître la mode, demande la collaboration de nombreux spécialistes, dont des graphistes, des directeurs artistiques, des rédacteurs et des photographes. Toutes ces personnes jouent un rôle important dans le processus créatif, et c'est la vision conjointe de toutes les disciplines réunies qui permet de produire des images percutantes.

Johanna Bonnevier
À la fois directrice artistique, graphiste et illustratrice, Johanna Bonnevier d'origine suédoise est installée dans le quartier est de Londres. Ses domaines de prédilection sont l'architecture, la culture et la mode, et ses projets vont de travaux papier en petit ou grand format, à des génériques de film en passant par des installations.

La expresión de la autoexpresión
Johanna Bonnevier

La industria de la moda es, ante todo, una cuestión de autoexpresión. En el mundo de la moda, el diseño gráfico equivale en muchos aspectos al acto de transmitir una idea de autoexpresión que pasa a ser una extensión de la propia moda: una visión de algo en lo que la persona puede transformarse. La publicidad y el grafismo de la moda se centran a menudo precisamente en aquello "en lo que podrías convertirte".
La moda consiste en avanzar hacia nuevas tendencias, hacia lo *siguiente*, y el diseño gráfico de moda nos exige hallar un delicado equilibrio entre lo que el cliente es y lo que quiere ser.
Desde luego, es más fácil decir esto que hacerlo –por más que existan varias maneras de lograrlo–, pero una cosa que tienen en común la mayoría de los diseños gráficos de la industria de la moda es la atención al detalle, algo muy necesario para destacar en medio de una corriente continua de información. Materiales, tipografía, ilustración y otros varios elementos son necesarios en la creación de una perfecta comunicación entre la marca y el cliente. En la moda, más a menudo que en las demás industrias, vemos un uso sobresaliente e innovador de los materiales impresos y las técnicas gráficas. El grafismo evoluciona al compás de la calidad, los materiales y el diseño de la ropa.
Los vídeos de moda, un medio en el que cada vez se emplean tecnologías más avanzadas y cantidades crecientes de tiempo y de dinero, se han hecho muy populares. El diseño gráfico para este género relativamente joven les plantea a los diseñadores nuevos retos y les abre modos de expresión diferentes.

Por su parte, las marcas de lujo ponen cada año el listón más alto en las pasarelas de moda de todo el mundo, con sus espacios de exhibición y con todo lo que los rodea, como, por ejemplo, las tarjetas de las invitaciones, elementos particularmente poderosos para que la marca pueda crear esa primera impresión tan importante. Esta atención al detalle, junto con una comunicación coherente que abarca todos los aspectos del diseño, es el factor decisivo para que una marca se haga notar dentro de ese torrente de informaciones en pugna por captar la atención del consumidor.

Durante la útima década, los medios digitales han ido ganando importancia en la comunicación de las marcas con los clientes. La frase "estilo de vida" ha entrado en todas las industrias, y en la de la moda más que en ninguna otra. Hay muchas marcas de moda que exploran un amplio espectro de medios como revistas, vídeo y redes sociales, siempre en busca de un enfoque del "estilo de vida" más amplio y que les permita destacar.

La creación de tan extraordinarios trabajos es casi siempre fruto de la colaboración de muchos creativos de talento. Diseñadores, directores de arte, copys y fotógrafos, entre otros, son elementos importantes en el proceso creativo, y la visión combinada procedente de sus respectivas disciplinas es la que crea un grafismo poderoso.

Johanna Bonnevier
Johanna Bonnevier es una directora de arte, diseñadora gráfica e ilustradora sueca residente en Londres. Trabaja principalmente en proyectos relacionados con la arquitectura, la cultura y la moda, que abarcan desde trabajos para la imprenta de pequeño y gran tamaño hasta créditos de películas e instalaciones.

A expressão da autoexpressão
Johanna Bonnevier

A indústria da moda é, antes de tudo, uma questão de autoexpressão. No mundo da moda, o design gráfico equivale, em muitos aspectos, ao ato de transmitir uma ideia de autoexpressão que passa a ser uma extensão da própria moda: uma visão de algo em que a pessoa pode se transformar.

A publicidade e os materiais gráficos da moda centram-se, com frequência, precisamente naquilo "em que você poderia se transformar". A moda consiste em avançar rumo a novas tendências, rumo ao *seguinte*, e o design gráfico de moda exige que cheguemos a um delicado equilíbrio entre aquilo que o cliente é e aquilo que deseja ser.

Naturalmente, é mais fácil falar do que fazer –mesmo que existam várias maneiras de consegui-lo–; mas há uma coisa que a maioria dos designs gráficos da indústria da moda têm em comum: é a atenção aos detalhes, algo muito necessário para ter destaque no meio de um fluxo contínuo de informações. Materiais, tipografia, ilustração e vários outros elementos são necessários na criação de uma perfeita comunicação entre a marca e o cliente. Na moda, mais frequentemente do que nas outras indústrias, verificamos um notável e inovador uso dos materiais impressos e das técnicas gráficas. Os materiais gráficos evoluem no ritmo da qualidade, dos materiais e do design das roupas.

Os vídeos de moda, uma mídia na qual se empregam tecnologias cada vez mais avançadas e investimentos crescentes de tempo e de dinheiro, estão se tornando muito populares. O design gráfico para este gênero relativamente jovem levanta novos desafios para os designers e abre para eles diferentes modos de expressão.

A cada ano que passa, as marcas de luxo elevam, por sua vez, o patamar das passarelas de moda no mundo inteiro, com seus espaços de exibição e com tudo ao seu redor como, por exemplo, os convites, elementos especialmente poderosos para que a marca possa criar essa primeira impressão tão importante. Essa atenção ao detalhe, juntamente com uma comunicação coerente, que abranja todos os aspectos do design, é fator decisivo para que uma marca sobressaia no meio dessa torrente de informações em disputa para captar a atenção do consumidor.

Durante a última década, a mídia digital tornou-se cada vez mais importante na comunicação entre as marcas e os clientes. A frase "estilo de vida" entrou em todas as indústrias, e na indústria da moda mais do que em todas as outras. Existem muitas marcas de moda que exploram uma ampla variedade de mídias como revistas, vídeos e redes sociais, sempre à procura de uma abordagem mais ampla do "estilo de vida", que lhes permita um maior destaque.

A criação de trabalhos tão extraordinários é, quase sempre, fruto da colaboração de muitos criadores de talento. Designers, diretores de arte, copys e fotógrafos, entre outros, são elementos importantes no processo criativo, e a visão combinada de suas respectivas disciplinas é o que cria materiais gráficos poderosos.

Johanna Bonnevier
Johanna Bonnevier é uma diretora de arte, designer gráfica e ilustradora sueca residente em Londres. Trabalha principalmente em projetos relacionados com a arquitetura, a cultura e a moda, que vão desde obras de impressão de tamanho pequeno ou grande até créditos de filmes e instalações.

Edwina Hörl nanikore

photography seiji shibuya model hikaru make-up: fyar (piccadilly) art direction
angato and special thanks to empoto, onodera, yuki iwasaki, reiko terada (disc
seiji shibuya hikaru brandtlund fyar, susanna (pbe', alex sondregger, anae, s
susanne fie, evelyn and markus (onscreen), alfred (otou san), all friends and t

"Nani Kore" (what is this?) is the theme for this collection. The concept is built on Edwina Hörl's multicultural background. She is mixing traditional European style with Japanese style.

As the name implies so+ba produced an object that makes you question the nature of the object and think "what is this?" The final product, when unfolded, reveals the collection catalogue in the form of a printed handkerchief. It is a nonsensical marriage of a given object with a surprising content.

EDWINA HÖRL - MIMI
CREATIVE DIRECTION/DESIGN: SO+BA
PHOTOGRAPHY: TOSHIKI SENOUE

"Mimi" represents a variety of migration themed words and ideas, such as mix and minority, as well as the literal interpretation of the Japanese word for "ear".

The global circulation of stylistic elements within fashion, stands in opposition to codified indigenous fashion. This conflict is made visible in the mimi collection. Symbols of mobility and contemporaneity are mixed with traditional motifs. Globalism, cultural networks, compulsory consumption, and the interchange between old and new are evaluated critically.

For the photo shoot, so+ba placed the models into alien surroundings.

For example: items of a woman's living room are placed with a model on public space in Harajuku where passersby are forced to deal with this forced conflation of private life and public space.

Another example: a man is photographed washing his laundry in an underground parking garage, his actions directly conflict with normal socially acceptable behavior within that defined space.

Using these photos, a sealed stack of cards with accompanying texts and graphs analyzing social nomadic trends and foreign populations of the world, were created.

Mi Mi

Hörl

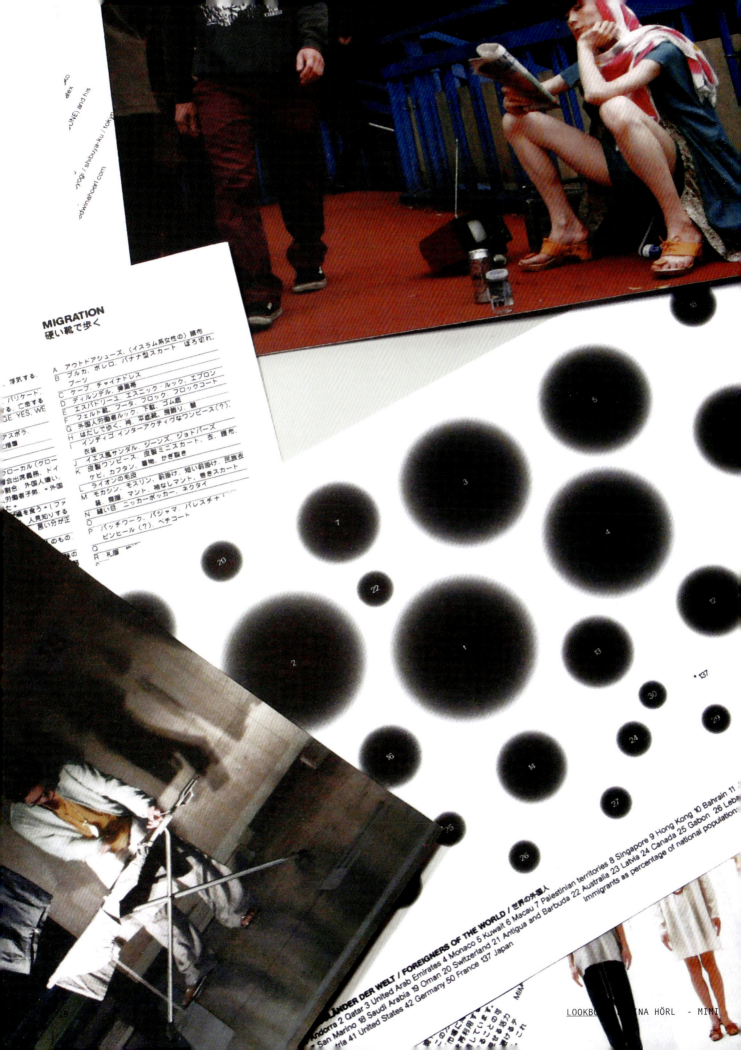

MIGRATION
硬い靴で歩く

A アウトドアシューズ、（イスラム系女性の）頭布
B ブルカ、ボレロ、バナナ型スカート、ぼろ切れ、
　ブーツ、チャイナドレス
C ケープ、チャイナドレス
D ディルンデル、薄襦袢
E エスパドリーユ、エスニック・ルック、エプロン
F フェルト靴、フータ、フロック、フロックコート
　ゴム底
G 外国人労働者ルック、下駄、裾飾り、裾
H はだしで歩く、肩、半長靴、腰飾りなワンピース（？）、
　衣装
J インディゴ インタラクティブなワンピース、ジョドパーズ
K イエス風サンダル、ジーンズ、皮製ミニスカート、衣、頭布、
　衣装
L ライオンの毛皮
M ケビ、カフタン、裾帯、かぎ裂き
N モカシン、モスリン、前掛け、短い前掛け、民族衣
　装、腰腰、マント、袖なしマント、巻きスカート
O 縫い目、ニッカーボッカー、ネクタイ
P パッチワーク、パジャマ、パレスチナ
　ピンヒール（？）、ペチコート
Q
R 礼服

LÄNDER DER WELT / FOREIGNERS OF THE WORLD / 世界の外国人
1 ... 2 Qatar 3 United Arab Emirates 4 Monaco 5 Kuwait 6 Macau 7 Palestinian territories 8 Singapore 9 Hong Kong 10 Bahrain 11 ... Andorra 2 Qatar ... San Marino 18 Saudi Arabia 19 Oman 20 Switzerland 21 Antigua and Barbuda 22 Australia 23 Latvia 24 Canada 25 Gabon 26 Leba... ...ria 41 United States 42 Germany 50 France 137 Japan
Immigrants as percentage of national population...

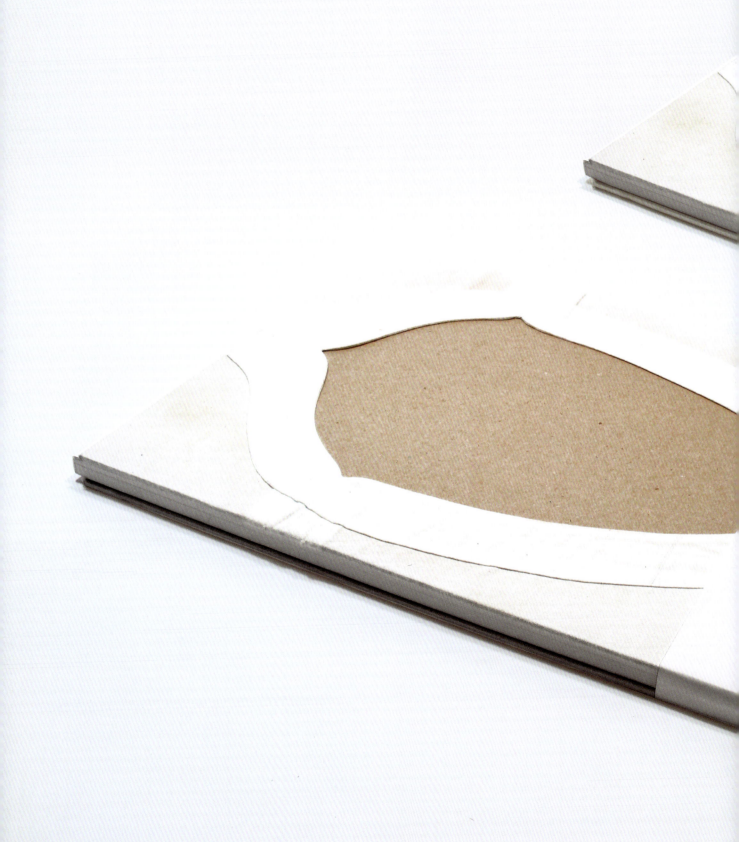

APPLICATION
FOR THE INTERNATIONAL PR PRIZE

EDWINA HÖRL
FEBRUARY 2009

Edwina Hörl

This book was made for the application for the international PR prize, Austria. The contents consist of Edwina Hörl's PR campaigns from 2005 to 2009. The cover is made of a garment collar.

EDWINA HÖRL - AAA
CREATIVE DIRECTION/PHOTOGRAPHY/DESIGN: SO+BA

"AAA" the theme for this collection, is created by using the abbreviation of "Anshin Anzen Anarchy".

"Anshin" in Japanese for peace of mind, "Anzen" for safety and security and "Anarchy" as a gateway to freedom in world dominated by the rich and powerful. "AAA" also stands for the highest country credit rating in the financial world.

For this collection so+ba organized a protest demonstration in Shibuya. The group of protesters where standing still several times in the middle of Tokyo's busiest crossing on a weekend. In every person lives an anarchist. In some corner of the mind sits the unwavering will to live and a spirit to fight for freedom of thought and expression. so+ba (re)conquer public space in the middle of the tyranny of systems.

THANKS TO ALL WHO TOOK PART IN THIS
PROJECT AND SUPPORTED IT WITH THEIR
K N O W - H O W   A N D   E N T H U S I A S M

a r t - d i r e c t i o n 7 e o r l a
/ art direction / alfons josef sonderburger
p h o t o g r a p h y   h i r o m i   s u g i u r a
s t y l i n g   h i r o m i   s u g i u r a
m a k e - u p   y o s h i e   s a s a k i (sylph)
model studio in shibuya maike, roger, mana
anarchista in shibuya kaya, kyoko, mana
shimura, yoko mukase, susanna baer, akitaka
takaya ueda, yuuki kaneko, ryusuke kase
m i y a m o t o ,   y u u k i   k a n e k o ,   r y u s u k e   k a s e
a s s i s t a n c e / r y u s u k e   k a s e
c o l l e c t i o n
p a t t e r n   sonoko kato, mitsunori tsuchiya
a s s i s t a n c e   s o n o k o ,   r y u s u k e   k a s e
y u u k i   k a n e k o ,   y o s h i a k i   k u n i i

thanks to takakura-san (resortcrafts) co ltd), ito-
san (curita) to il) (atelier leo), nakakawa-san (maiey
co ltd), kato-san & jyoema-san (textile kuro co ltd)

テ— マ yoshiaki kunii, masanori tsuchiya, satine
muriele, karin ruprechter, hineko kassgi,
asuman mert, hiromi sugiura, yoehie
sasaki, maike, roger, kaya, kyoco,
mana shimura, yoko mukasa,
chikako iguchi, takaya ueda, akitaka
miyamoto, hiroko ito, susanna
baer, alex sonderegger, sanae ota
thanks to [dune] & [nidj]-teams

thanks to younai-san and hiro-san   様

伝票 No.129

税込合計金額

"Never give up" is the follow up of the "Namida" (tears) collection which Edwina Hörl created after the big triple disaster in Tohoku, East Japan. Edwina Hörl's cloths are produced in Tohoku. This collection is a tribute to all the factory workers in Tohoku, struggling with daily life.

The icon for this collection is a dragonfly. In Japan dragonflies are symbols of courage, strength, and happiness. They often appear in art and literature, especially haiku. Beyond this, "Akitsushima" one of Japan's historical names, is an archaic form meaning "Dragonfly islands". This is attributed to a legend in which Japan's mythical founder, Emperor Jinmu, was bitten by a mosquito, which was then promptly eaten by a dragonfly.

EDWINA HÖRL - KURONEKO
CREATIVE DIRECTION/DESIGN: SO+BA
PHOTOGRAPHY: SEIJI SHIBUYA

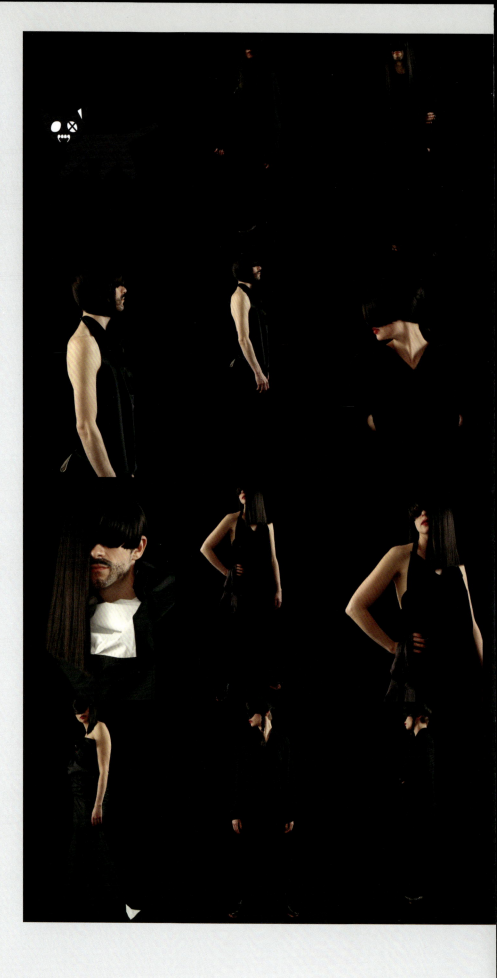

Kuroneko (black cat) – all black, you can
distinguish nothing: matt black, glossy black,
velvety black, jet black, pure black ...

The whole collection was designed in black using
different materials. The black dressed models
where positioned in front of a black background.
Their eyes were covered by their hair, and faux
cat eyes were positioned where the models' eyes
would be.

The cloths where not visible anymore, they have
been blending into the background, and only some
skin parts and the "cat eyes" flashed out. Fashion
disappeared.

The fashion show was held in an unfinished
underground subway station in Osaka. It was all
dark and each spectator had a small flashlight to
check the models and dresses.

Black cats are also considered good luck in Japan
and it is believed that a lady who owns a black cat
will have many suitors.

LOOKBOOK EDWINA HÖRL - KURONEKO

EDWINA HÖRL - PIRATERY
CREATIVE DIRECTION/DESIGN: SO+BA
PHOTOGRAPHY: LEO PELLEGATTA

Piracy is a multifaceted problem in both contemporary fashion and contemporary culture: When is something (an) original? When is something a copy? Is everything a copy of a copy of a copy? Is culture a big endless copy-machine in which people just re-create?

so+ba created a long, narrow, accordion-folded promotional catalogue that mimics Japanese "Harisen" ("slapping fan" or "war fan"), a prop that has a long tradition in Japanese comedy to hit fellow comedians on stage. On one side of the fan, all the models garbed in the collection's clothing are chaotically layered in a hybrid digital/analog collage that simultaneously questions and reveals notions of piracy and representation. For the exhibition we created a pirate-themed graphic installation with 140 A3 black and white photocopies. Images of pirates movies were pirated to create a visual and conceptual feedback loop on the notions of piracy.

Drawing references from fictional Japanese giant monsters, the direct mailer was designed in the format of a newspaper announcing the descendent of Giants, to launch the new Japanese labels from retailer Blackjack for Spring/Summer 09. On first look, the direct mailer appears like a pseudo piece of newspaper akin to old Japanese comics. Upon peering inside, the piece unveils its real form by introducing the retailer's exhilarating assembly of fashion industry's rising design collectives.

CAMPAIGN BLACKJACK DIRECT MAILER

EASTIE EMPIRE LOOKBOOK AW12
DESIGN: TWO TIMES ELLIOTT

Eastie Empire is a men's clothing brand from London. They pride themselves on producing tailored, gentlemen wear that plays homage to days gone by.

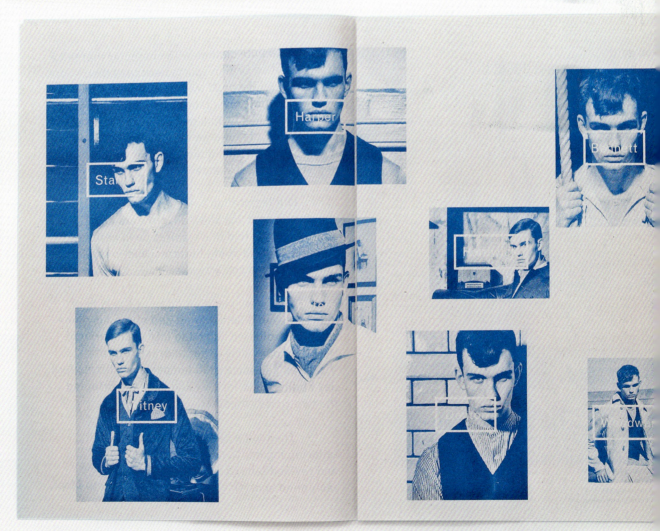

GUERILLA STORE

hosted by
creativespace.at

LISKA by Thomas
Kirchgrabner

AWARDS 09

8
magazine

festival for fashion
& photography
28/5–6/6
2008

festival and publication
by Unit F
büro für mode

Die Presse

This is a professionally designed high-class magazine with a double use: it announces the festival for fashion and photography; and it is a special-interest magazine for Austrian fashion design and fashion photography. The challenge was to create a medium for three genres: fashion magazine, programme information and special interest magazine. The outcome was a 56-page journal, based on an elaborate graphic concept that merges the genres by providing each of them with a specific area for presentation. By following the structure the reader is led through the festival magazine-without mistaking it for a standard programme brochure.

& photography
festival für Wien

IM NETZ

9 festival Shortcuts – www.9festival.at
Der Newsletter von Unit F informiert täglich über die Veranstaltungen im Rahmen des Festivals.

9 festival Blog – 9festival.stylishkidsinriot.com
– www.stylekingdom.com
Die Fashionblogger Stefan Urschler/SKIR und Maria Ratzinger/Stylekingdom berichten auf ihren Portalen von allen Festivalorten.

9 festival Mobile Guide – http://9.unlike.net
Um den Service für die Festivalbesucher zu verbessern, werden Programm, Locations und Tours des Festivals als Mobile City Guide aufbereitet.

9 festival Online Store – www.notjustalabel.com
Mit der Einführung ihres Online Stores bietet NJAL, die Londoner Online-Plattform für zeitgenössisches Modedesign, erstmals Mode österreichischer Designer/innen an.

9 festival Online Lookbook – www.creativespace.at
Stylingtipps und Outfits aller im Guerilla Store vertretenen Labels.

DANK AN:

Masa Adams, Anna Aichinger, Birgit Aichinger, Niko Alm, Imran Amed, Gerhild Amerer, Karl Ammerer, Isabelle Aout, Antoine Asseraf, Gerald Bast, Jürgen Bauer, Sergei Benedetter, Christiane Bertolini, Martin Blank, Andrew Blyszak, Willi und Edwige Brundlmayer, Renate Brauner, Céline Brigg, Birgit Brodner, Tony Cederteg, Darius und Eva Chegini, Theresa Dallio Haubner, Barbara Irma Denk, Samuel Drira, Markus Ebner, Carl Peter Echtermeijer, Andrea Eckert, Hannes Eder, Alice Egger, Brigitta Fiala, Katherine Fiedler, Klaus Fritsch, Alexander Geringer, Yoan Gonfond, Ruth Goubran, Hilda Grandits, Rene Habermacher, Stefan Hackel, Yvonne Hasler, Albert Handler, Ursula Hauer, Nikolaus Hauer, Julia Herbster, Elisabeth Herdin, David Herman, Natascha Hochenegg, Susanna Hoffmann-Ostenhof, Barbara Hofleitner, Hans Holler, Anita Hörburger, Florian Horwath, Martin Hotzeneder, Ciuo Hu, Brigitte Jank, Lisa Joham, Christian Kemmler, Norbert Kettner, Isabelle Kiener, Roswitha Kladnig, Michaela Knapp, Dorothea Köb, Birgitt Kohl, Sylvia Kolenz, Andreas Kristof, Yogesh Kumar, Andreas Lackner, Jasmin Ladenhaufen, Bibiane Lanner-Yeganehfar, Gernot Leonhartsberger, Philip List, Tamara Lorenzi, Klaus Mühlbauer, Leopold Machacek, Vijai Maheshwari, Andreas Mailath-Pokorny, Claudia Maschke, Marc Mathos, Gabor Merö, Karin Neuhold, Elisabeth Noever-Günthör, Olga Okunev, Kosmas Pavlos, Diane Pernet, Ruudi Peters, Petar Petrov, Constantin Peytuss, Claus Philipp, Martin Pieper, Peter Pilotto, Ute Ploner, Lili Pliokova, Stefan Pollak, Christian Pöttler, Renate Rapf, Maria Ratzinger, Anouk Rehorek, Ariane Reither, Werner Rodlauer, Doris Rothauer, Valerie Sadik, Christian Schantl, Peter H. Schindler, Katha Schinkinger, Christian Schlager, Claudia Schmied, Doris Schretzmayer, Robin Schulie, Anja Seipenbusch, Birgit Seiwald, Stefan Siegel, Claudia Six, Gian Paolo Spadola, Carola Stütz, Markus Strasser, Sybille Straubinger, Karoline Strobl, Christian Suppan, Christoph Thun-Hohenstein, Astrid Tichy, Desaree Trechl-Sturghh, Jasmin Turek, Stefan Urschler, Rita Vitorelli, Klaus Peter Vollmann, Magdalena Vukovic, Klaus Vyhnalek, Jutta Wacht, Tom Wallmann, Andrea Wendler, Ole Weinreich, Jork Weismann, Christina Werner, Brigitte B. Winkler, Waltraud Wolf, alle Unterstützer und die vielen helfenden Hände …

AFA–AUSTRIA FASHION AWARDS 09
Die Nominierten

Christina Steiner

MODEPREIS DES BUNDESMINISTERIUMS FÜR
UNTERRICHT, KUNST UND KULTUR
Ali Zedtwitz

SA 6/6 – Symposium – **go international Talks** – FASHION 2.0 – Fashion Blogger Day – Fash Clash: Discussing the Digital Controversy – Bulgarisches Kulturinstitut Haus Wittgenstein – Parkgasse 18, 1030 Wien – Beginn: 16h, vorauss. Ende: 19h

GO INTERNATIONAL TALKS
FASHION 2.0
– Fashion Blogger Day

JULIA KNOLLE

DIANE PERNET

IMRAN AMED

SUSIE BUBBLE

JOHANNES THUMFART

BIRGITT KOHL

BZR LOOKBOOK AW11

ART DIRECTION/GRAPHIC DESIGN: DESIGNBOLAGET
PHOTOGRAPHY: SACHA MARIC

BZR is a sub-label of fashion brand Bruuns Bazaar targeting younger people.

For the lookbook of A/W 2011, Designbolaget came up with an unconventional format — a poster-like newspaper in A2. Layout-wise, every spread is treated as a separate composition in itself. This publication features more an editorial approach than a classic, streamlined lookbook. The large format provides plenty of space for both the seasonal collection and the core brand values of BZR.

autumn winter
'10 –
'11

annemie
verbeke
—

Todorov (top)

Design and photography for Annemie Verbeke's catalogues. Catalogues of every season has the same dimensions, but each time differs in paper / folding / graphical approach.

Titos (top) / Petro (legging) / Aude (belt) / Alexis (cap)   Dinky (dress) / Alice (parka) / Alissa (furcollar)   Douglas (dress)   Domino (dress) / Alissa (furcollar)   Mandel (top) / Stern (skirt)

Bell (blouse) / Adler (cardi) / Adami (belt) / Popescu (pant)   Baker (blouse) / Astoria (scarf) / Popescu (pant)   Tsar (top) / Sinclair (skirt) / Altochad (socks)   Dorisgen (dress) / Peter (scarf)   Maxwell

Deecull (dress)   Dolina (dress) / Acosta (cardi)   Todorus (top) / Titos (t-shirt)   Dolina (dress) / Arba (socks)   Das (dress) / Arno (cape) / Altoche

'11

DIAZ dress / AUSTIN scarf

MAXAE cream cardi / DAN dress

CONCHITA crochet top / POUND pant

CANYON sweater / SKY skirt / AIR knitted hat

MAUREEN knitted dress / AME belt

DORA black & white dress

JANICE striped jacket / SKY striped skirt

MANA sunflower cardi / STRAND shirt knavel

COSTA top / SUN skirt / ASTRID socks

COLORADO minidress

CARÉE woven and knitted cardi

SEPPA tic silk & cork denim dress

DANCE green shirtdress

PAILLE pant / CLAUDIA knitted top

DELFINA teeshirtdress

MARFA knitted top / SKY skirt

The catalogue for Cortana's AW12/13 collection is a newsprint publication that, even though using a low budget printing technique, presents a refined and contemporary design. Contradicting the usual size of a newspaper, Folch Studio designed a small-size publication where photography is given highest prominence and Cortana's collection design is enhanced.

Nostalgic typographic identity for fashion retailer Skirt. Founded developed a set of supporting elements to use as a key part of the retailers branding. The shapes were taken from the negative spaces of the Skirt marque. Logo, imagery and brand shapes all were brought together for use in the marketing literature.

SKIRT
BOUTIQUE

Paul & Joe Sister

Autumn/Winter 2010—
New Season Highlights

Ossinctur, quid que magnam fugia doluptunibus enit inctati umenias vellon dero bea voles nonsequost larch illorit iduciur eicabo. Neque commi ut volupta tinctas pa con nis recepelo bitatum reratia iscipsa operebensmi. Nodi vitatur atiat quo fecullvet alit eseneperium que pro quis dempossedit aut odis ullupta temporibus cust ab ipsam autempo stiusap erorit.

Alumqui buscia placcupta volorumqui quosl, sitiando dis eumendem faecatem ad mo venisquodis restemp oreped quae rempedit elendre unturehent ea quam et por sit am dis sus quibea dolorion revciur si dem ut volupta fiaepfur alit, con re comvim liquaspedis eatatibeat issuntem eium oum utem faccabium acitatione quam, sum laborepptis sim venices eos eos rem alis qu dolorep elignietur rerspe nem fugia pellaces et porunlut.

Fas enit, earumen isecero vitatia simonctatur accus quddiS nvendem ab is vel ipsa delibus quo quia comma eum consed que nobitiaei nmiili re aut occatie nullvas ilibusam incae vollecto tatius as aborem nilsi num, volo dolres aut voloreunime vero conectaquunt iqv veriqua.

Nat faci ilaci arum ent aceaquaespero motuptate oren demquam, am eatem aceptatur? Faccus ipis ea idero corenmodi ipsum rae. Corionecha dem qus essequo cusam doflacera doluptiore pri venta simaginihil il incti sus sum hariamus invelis dolut delentio. Itaquisteque volut omnnos ma dotor suridae nation consequ at ni doluptaque nulliqu nobis cuscill issenda mens et anis et eskis qiatur alic tem quis etut dolorpor mos apid magninip oren nimus volor sunt, officia sin cima aut pra doloreptat poreceperro disserum que vendit.

Right—
Ilumu sofia verdige lis ele et quas doloreo non perio. Eicrig Vilulgvinha ato af quis doloreo non perio. £279

Tel 0191 221 0234 — Email info@skirtboutique.co.uk — Visit skirtboutique.co.uk

SKIRT BOUTIQUE

Tel 0191 221 0234
Email info@skirtboutique.co.uk
skirtboutique.co.uk

19 Highbridge,
Newcastle upon Tyne NE1 1EW

—Up to 70% off instore and online now
—Get the best of summer for less

PAUL & JOE SISTER
MBYM
DANSK
ELLA MOSS
IVANA HELSINKI
CHEAP MONDAY
KATE SHERIDAN

b+ab is a Hong Kong based fashion label, under the I.T stable of brands. Drawing inspiration from the collection itself and the whimsical and surreal aspects of the brand, the Spring/Summer campaign centered around the concept of "hunter gatherer". An imaginative, fantasy world of the unpredictable and bizarre depicted through the photography of Marcelo Krasilcic and the illustration of Dylan Martorell.

AGENCY: BUREAU COLLECTIVE
DESIGN: OLLIE SCHAICH, RUEDI ZÜRCHER
PHOTOGRAPHY: MAURICE HAAS

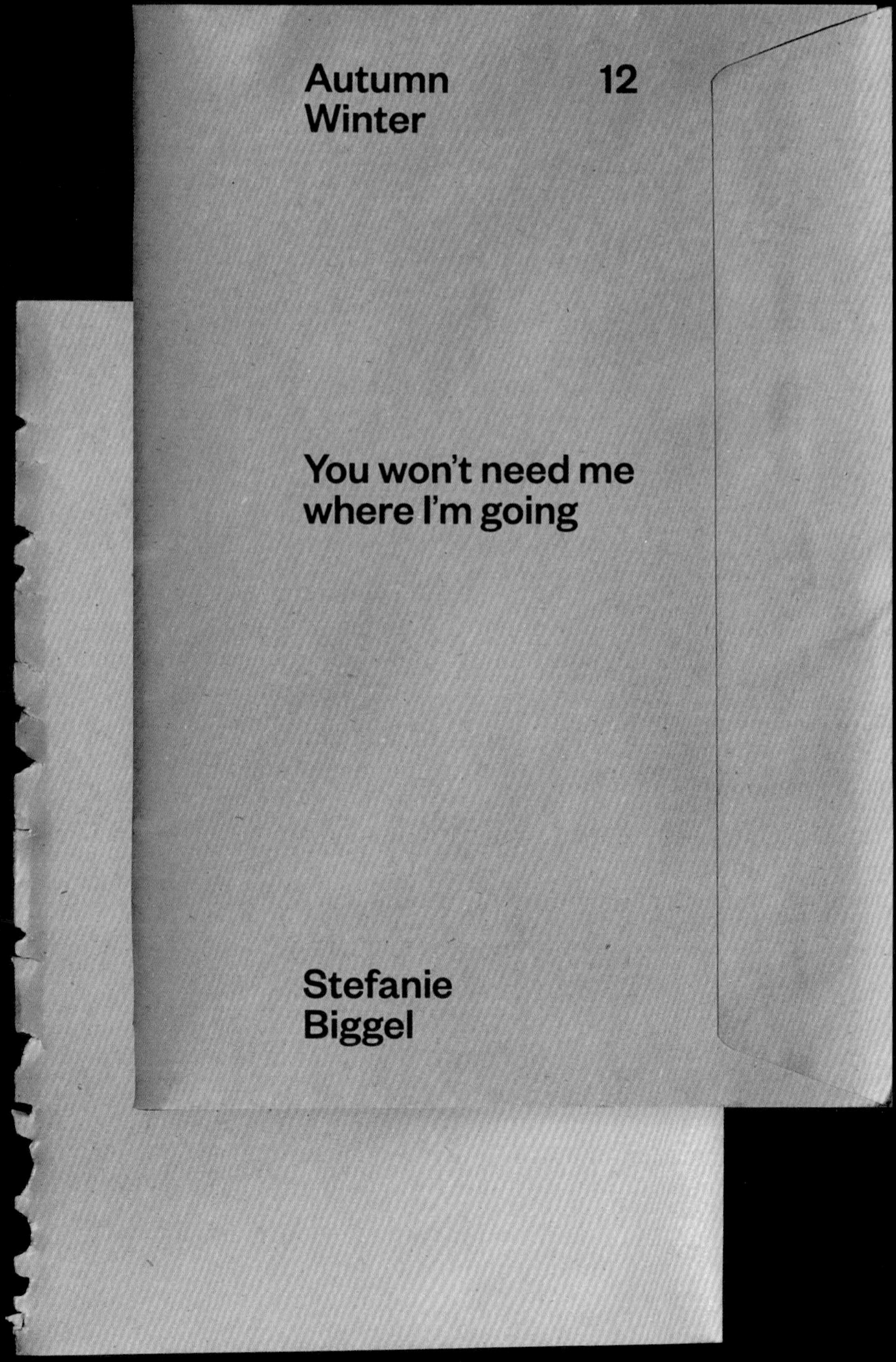

Autumn   **12**
Winter

You won't need me
where I'm going

Stefanie
Biggel

Stefanie Biggel is a fashion designer based in Zurich, Switzerland. Bureau
Collective designed the lookbook for her autumn/winter 2012 collection.
create a natural feeling, the book is printed on a bulky paper and is bound
with a thread into a folded recycling protective bag.

Autumn
Winter

12

You won't need me
where I'm going

Stefanie
Biggel

Photography:
Maurice Haas

Model:
Helena Roell

Hair & Make-Up:
Linda Sigg
Lena Fleischer

Styling:
Oriana Tundo

Graphic Design:
Bureau
Collective

stefaniebiggel.com

STUDIO NEWWORK had designed Spring / Summer 2011 & 2012 invitations for a NY-based menswear brand J.SABATINO.

Location:
Honey Space
148 11th Avenue
Btw. 21st & 22nd
New York, NY 10011

Date / Time:
Monday February 14, 2011
From 5:30
To 7:00

RSVP:
jsabatino@
modepublicrelations.com

J.SABATINO
SS12

PASSED BY
J S
SS12

VI
AUTUMN/WINTER 2012

CONTACT
PHONG CHI LAI
ROOM 517, 37 SWANSTON ST
MELBOURNE, VICTORIA, 3000
AUSTRALIA
TELEPHONE: +61 431000167
EMAIL: INFO@PHONGCHILAIHANDCRAFT.COM

CREDITS
PHOTOGRAPHY: PETER RYLE | CONTACT@PETERRYLEPHOTOGRAPHY.COM
GRAPHIC DESIGN: LATITUDE GROUP | WWW.LATITUDEGROUP.COM.AU

Phong Chi Lai's eponymous footwear label presents itself with a skillful artisan aesthetic and an exceptional crafted quality. Working closely with Phong, Latitude was commissioned to produce and develop a look that reflects the nature of these thoughtful and hand-made products. The result is a combination of craft and design that evokes the spirit of the brand. The identity evolved into an array of foil blocks and leather emboss stamps, with the photography directed to look at the footwear as art.

VI
AUTUMN/WINTER
2012

SC KYOTO TO TOKIO
GRAPHIC DESIGN: LUCA FATTORE
FASHION ACCESSORIES: SARA CEOLDO

Kyoto to Tokio is the second project of Sara Ceoldo. It tells about the dichotomy between Kyoto and Tokyo and their evolution after the second world war. The cities inspire two different routes that define two design approaches. The Booklet has mirror-contents that remembers manga type of reading.

N°1
weekender

Length	→	69,50 cm
Width	↗	23,00 cm
Height	↑	33,50 cm

04

N°2
pochette

Length	→	47,50 cm
Width	↗	32,50 cm
Height	↑	10,50 cm

05

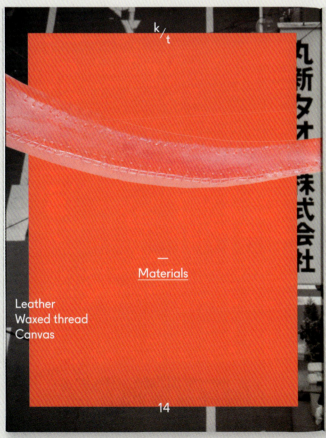

—
Materials

Leather
Waxed thread
Canvas

14

Tokio 東京

35° 41′ 22.22″ N, 139° 41′ 30.12″ E

Surface	2 187,66 km²
Inhabitants	13 185 502 (2011)
Density	6 027,22 ab./km²

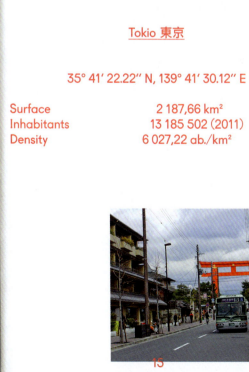

15

TMX's AW11/12 catalogue was designed
based on the idea of presenting the collection
as a special object different from the typical
fashion catalogues.

A box containing two refined publications,
with binding and stamping details, provides an
experience of discovery of TMX's collection,
and providing the brand with a contemporary
and unique voice.

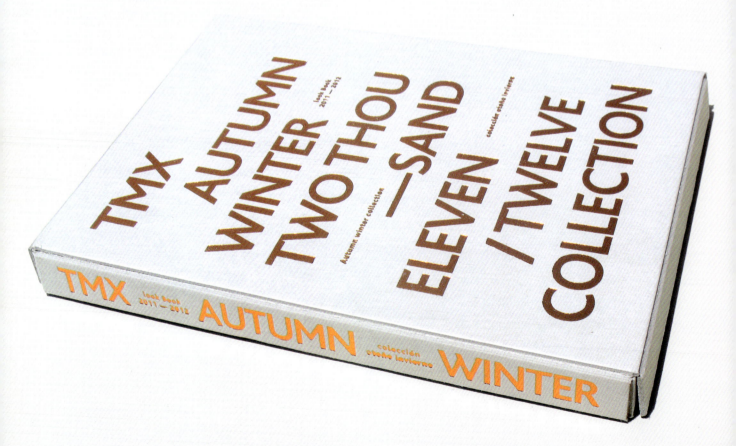

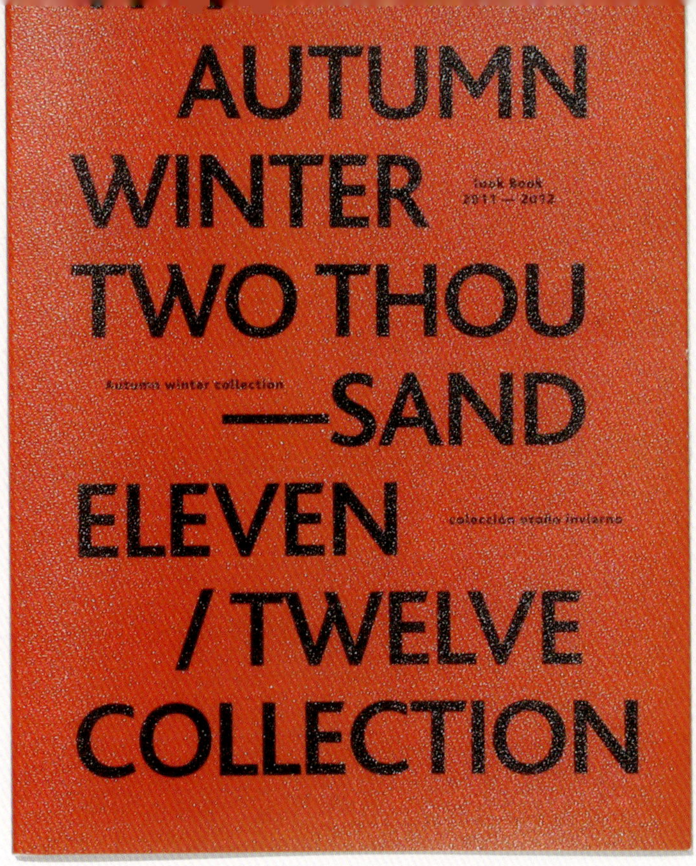

AUTUMN WINTER TWO THOU —SAND ELEVEN / TWELVE COLLECTION

look Book
2011 — 2012

Autumn winter collection

colección otoño invierno

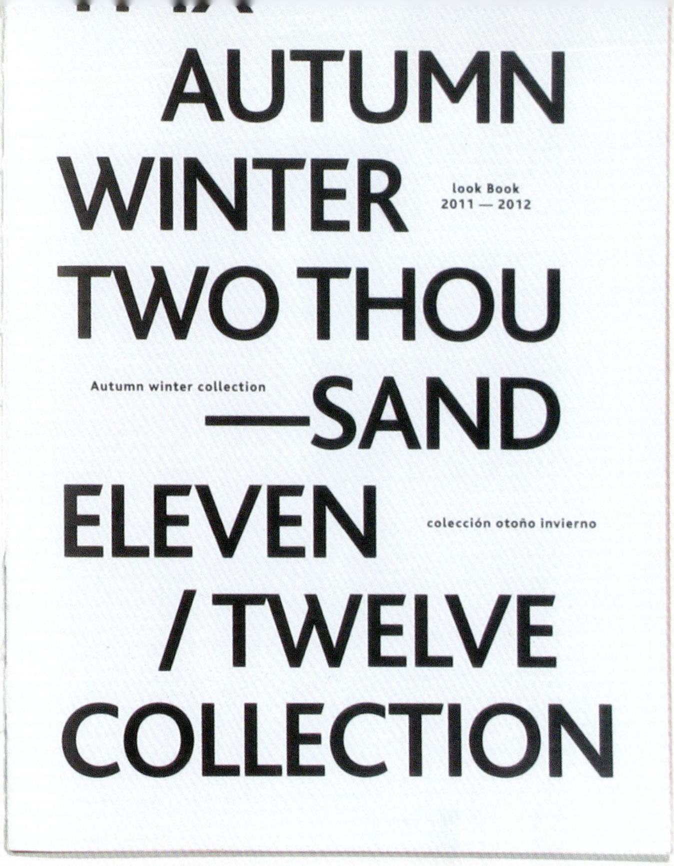

AUTUMN WINTER TWO THOU —SAND ELEVEN / TWELVE COLLECTION

look Book
2011 — 2012

Autumn winter collection

colección otoño invierno

**TMX AUT
— UMN WINTER TWO
THAUSAND ELE
—VEN AND TWELVE
COLLECTION**

01   02   03   07   08

TMX AUTUMN WINTER TWO THOU —SAND ELEVEN

look Book
2011 — 2012

Autumn winter collection

colección otoño invierno

PREEN
BY
THORNTON BREGAZZI

SS 2012 'Virginia'

P R E E N
BY
THORNTON BREGAZZI

Spring Summer 2012

Monday 12th September at 11am
IAC Building, 555 West 18th Street
New York, NY 10011

RSVP
E. preen@bpcm.com T. 646 380 3806

Name _____

Row _____ *Seat* _____

One of the main fabric prints for this season contained coloured pixel squares, and so Studio Thomson focused on this aspect as a starting point for the design of the SS12 show material. They presented various different configurations of the pixels but after discussing the designs with Preen they decided to go with a very pared down invitation with a simple row of pixels along the top of the card, reminiscent of the rows of colour boxes you see on printers proofs. They chose a square format for the invitation which was then sent out in multicoloured square envelopes based on the colours of the pixels. For the look book cover they revealed the entire pixel pattern, and combined traditional catwalk shots with reportage style images shot from the perspective of the audience to give the look book a fresh appeal.

VANESSA GATE SS13

DESIGN: AILSA MARRS
PHOTOGRAPHY: RYAN DAVIES
LOGO: JONATHAN FINCH

SPRING / SUMMER COLLECTION

VANESSA GATE

SPRING / SUMMER COLLECTION

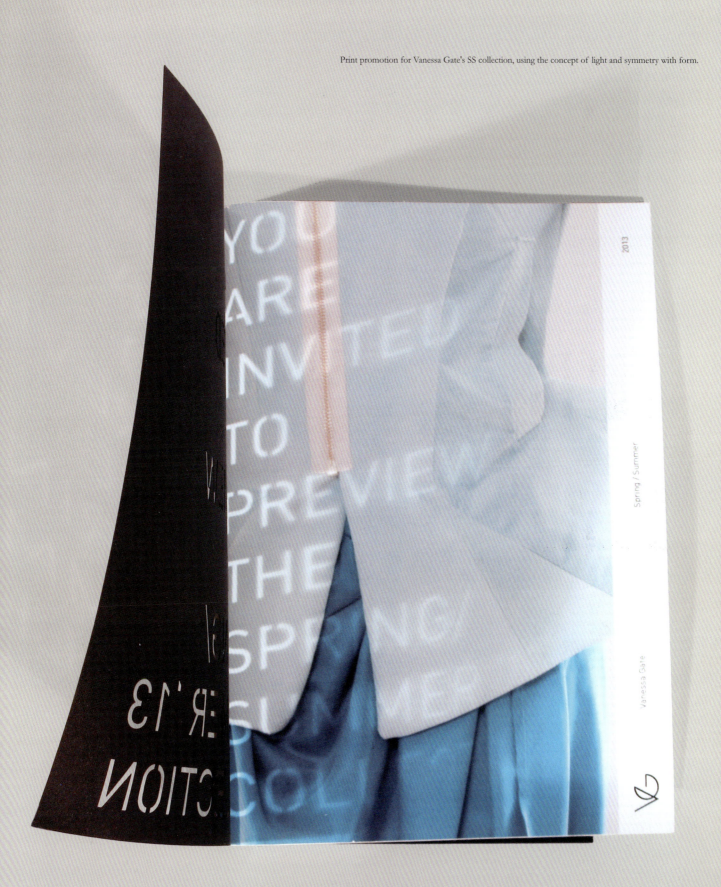

SITA MURT IT'S SHOWTIME, FW10/11
DESIGN: CLASE BCN
ART DIRECTION: CLASE BCN
WATERCOLOUR: CLARET SERRAHIMA
PHOTOGRAPHY: TXEMA YESTE
STYLING: CLAUDIA ENGLMANN

A catalogue that unshamedly mixes fashion images with water colour textures to reflect the brand's characteristic interest in and links to the world of art.

CENTRAL SAINT MARTINS, LOST IN LACE

CLIENT: CENTRAL SAINT MARTINS COLLEGE, LONDON
GRAPHIC DESIGN/ILLUSTRATION: STUDIOTHOMSON
PROJECT COORDINATION: JO SIMPSON

Lost in Lace

Olivia Oram

Thanks to

Jochen Braun
Tim Meara
Helmert Robbertsen
Patricia Williams
Annie Wilshaw at Premier Models
AMCK Models

Models
Pilar & Vanessa at Premier Models
Ysham at AMCK Models
Alannah Louet Feisser
Martin Wang

Project coordinator – Jo Simpson
Graphic Design – StudioThomson

Anna Parra Melendez

StudioThomson were approached by the Central Saint Martins Foundation course to design a brochure to showcase the work created by students on the styling for fashion and textiles pathway. The work was inspired by the Lost in Lace exhibition shown at the Birmingham Museum and Art Gallery, and so they created a graphic identity based on lace making diagrams and used it to frame the information within the brochure. As the project was to be self financed by the students they proposed a simple cost effective newspaper format which allowed each student a single page to showcase their work.

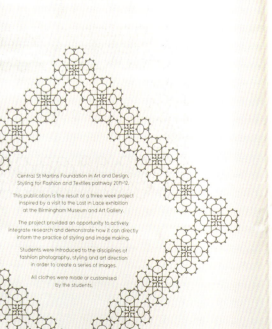

Central St Martins Foundation in Art and Design,
Styling for Fashion and Textiles pathway 2011-12.

This publication is the result of a three week project
inspired by a visit to the Lost in Lace exhibition
at the Birmingham Museum and Art Gallery.

The project provided an opportunity to actively
integrate research and demonstrate how it can directly
inform the practice of styling and image making.

Students were introduced to the disciplines of
fashion photography, styling and art direction
in order to create a series of images.

All clothes were made or customised
by the students.

Essie Buckman

izes graceful
on with a dis-
emporary edge
gh masterful
ality fabrics
ouettes and a
e of wearable
design Noir

Noir epitomi
sophisticatio
tinctive conte
created throu
tailoring, qu
slender silho
unique sense
and lasting

Noir epitomizes
graceful sophistication
with a distinctive contemporary edge,
created through masterful tailoring,
quality fabrics, slender silhouettes
and a unique sense of wearable and lasting design

No
so
tin
cr
tai
sle
un
and lasting design Noir

noir

Art Direction and Design for Noir Campaign Book SS1

ey / Blue
ey / Green

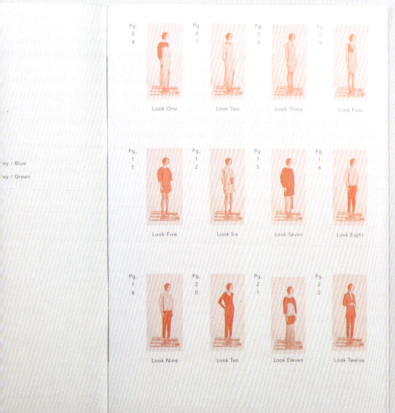

With this lookbook, Thursday Sunday wanted to capture the simplicity yet well crafted designs in a way which reflected their design principals and ideals.

Top:
Hand Knitted
Contrast Jumper
—
PWK4016

Bottom:
Asymmetrical Fold
Skirt
—
PWS4004

Pg
0
16

Top:
Raw Fringe Jumper
—
PWT4007

Bottom:
High Waisted
Contrast Pant
—
PWB4002

Pg
0
17

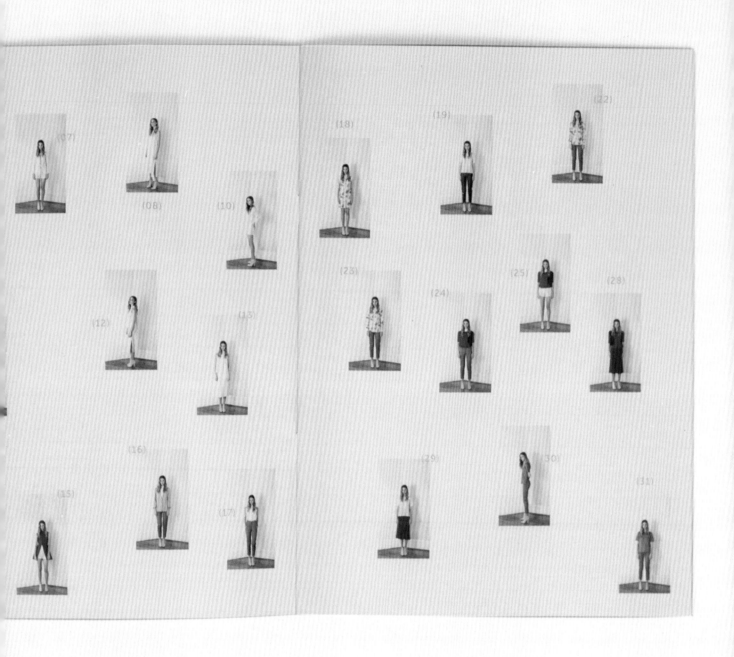

The design reflects the simple nature and subtle details that Thursday Sunday is known for. Using colours from their collection helped visually tie the concept together. The cover was cut in half to give imagery high contrast and slow reveal to their SS13 collection.

RED BY WOLVES
CREATIVE DIRECTION: MATTHEW SCHOFIELD
DESIGN: DAVID WELLER AND SUNNY PARK
PHOTOGRAPHY: DOH LEE

THIS IS OUR KINGDOM
www.redbywolves.com

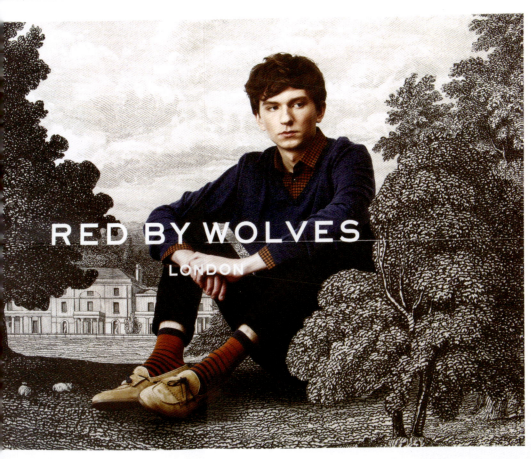

THIS IS OUR KINGDOM
www.redbywolves.com

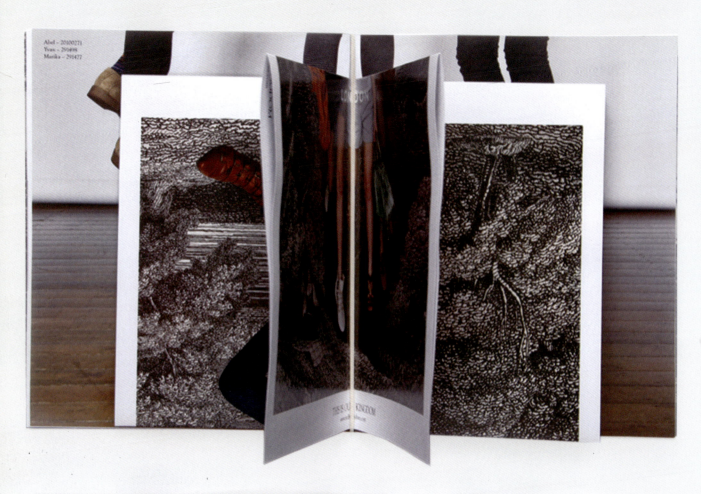

Abel – 20100271
Yvan – 291498
Marika – 291472

Abel – 20100271
Yvan – 291498
Marika – 291472

Complete rebranding of up-and-
coming shoe label, including
a lookbook showcasing both
new season and classic Red By
Wolves shoes. Building on brand's
established reputation for quality,
tradition and classic English styling,
the ad campaign set the shoes amid
an enchanting Lilliputian world
created from vintage etchings. Two
posters were loosely folded in the
centre spread..

THIS IS OUR KINGDOM
www.redbywolves.com

Art direction and graphic design for Mads Nørgaard campaign books SS13.

MADS
NØRGAARD
COPENHAGEN

WOMAN SPRING 2013 COLLECTION

GOLDE
CLASSI

MADS
NØRGAARD
COPENHAGEN

JEANS SPRING 2013 COLLECTION

MADS
NØRGAARD
COPENHAGEN

MAN SPRING 2013 COLLECTION

FRANCZ
MELBOURNE // AUSTRALIA

M/ TWISTED LEATHER JACKET
Available in Black

M/ METAL DRESS
...ted Edition

M/ METAL SHIRT
Limited Edition

M/ SPINAL LEATHER JACKET

M/ SPINAL DENIM JACKET

0430 049 396 // FRANCZ.COM.AU
by Geoffrey Haining

M/ FLAK JACKET
Limited Edition

Francz is a boutique Melbourne fashion label, made up of hand treated fabrics that are washed, beaten and treated to achieve a unique look for these handcrafted pieces. The brand blurs the line between male and female, contrasting strong, hard edged masculine materials against flowing feminine curves in their unique androgynous style. The clothing is inspired by military propaganda and subcultures throughout history—and the idea of belonging.

Inklab created the tall, sharp logotype to complement the military and punk undertones of the clothing, combined with a simplified colour palette. This concept was followed through the stationery and lookbook, with condensed typography versus a flowing serif.

The aim of this book was to produce an original and eye-catching piece of work using unconventional materials in a experimental way.

"'If a tree falls in a wood and no one was there to hear it, does it make a sound?', is a philosophical proverb that provokes questions regarding the knowlegde of reality and observation. Censcure explores this concept and extends its subject matter to cover censorship, whether it exists and in what way we are able to censor ourselves.

This book is an extension of this trend and it too creates new pathways of visiblity through the materials it made from and the way it has been constructed. Through the composition of the book the eye is forced to see thing as we want it to, blurred, sectioned and hidden."

JOSEFINSTRID AW12

AGENCY: DALSTON CREATIVE
DESIGN/ART DIRECTION: SOFIA DARKE AND MAGNUS DARKE
PHOTOGRAPHY: SARAH AND PAULINA
STYLING: TEREZA ORTIZ

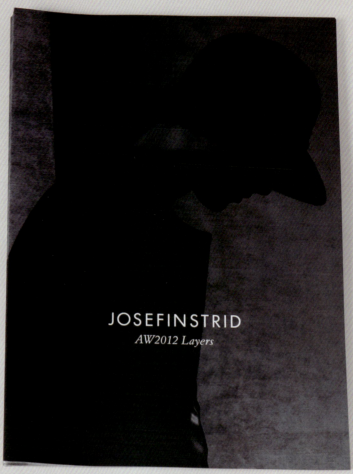

Design and art direction for fashion designer Josefinstrid AW12. This
included art direction of collection images and also design, concept and
production of lookbook, postcards and posters. As well as that Dalston
produced the digital backdrop for the catwalk show at Stockholm
Fashion Week.

AW2012 Layers

This collection is about reflection, stopping and thinking about the past, the present and the future. What has been done and how does it affect what comes next?
We read through the reviews from last season, what was our strengths and which skills do we need to develop further? Our muse was very important from the beginning, joining us in the process from the start. Who are we? Who do we want to be? What is our design program?

The designer's time in NYC became a wake-up call. The mission was all clear and after one afternoon at Whitney Museum she was ready to start.

The designer's aim is to investigate and explore the masculinity in menswear and how it can be bent in various directions.

LAYERS | CITIES | HOUSES | HEAVINESS | SHARPNESS | SHADES | CONSTRUCTION | TRADITION | A LIGHT |

Looks AW2012

Looks AW2012

Composed of mainly blacks, Misomber Nuan's collections are reflections of emptiness and voids; the promise of happenings, emotions and a dream to touch others through their experimental creations. The various promotional literature created for Misomber Nuan are all directed to express their experimental approach towards materials and fabrics.

For his lookbook, inspired by distressed leather used by Misomber Nuan; the cover was smeared with paint & ink to create a distressed texture and also to reflect the brand's artisanal qualities.

For the initial promo mailer, the client wanted an article that was interesting and effective which resulted in the development of a self-enclosed mailer.

MHL. CARRIER BAG
DESIGN: STUDIOSMALL AND MARGARET HOWELL TEAM IN JAPAN

Inspired by the construction of industrial potato bags, the MHL. carrier bags were produced in the
white single sided brown kraft paper sewn at the base for added strength.

Collection lookbook printed as a newspaper to reflect the utilitarian nature of the Margaret Howell MHL. collection.

5

JELLY SHOE
The Ablett family business began by manufacturing rubber soles for the Northampton shoe trade. Their first jelly shoes were produced in response to the declining shoe industry. We've discovered their original mould and had it re-polished to produce the authentic jelly shoe – childhood memories on the beach revived.

1

2

WEEKEND BAG
This bag is made from a rainproof canvas normally used for sails and is manufactured by Aiguille, an outdoor equipment specialist in the Lake District. All trims are carefully selected and sourced in the UK. All bags in this range have poppers to attach an MHL Pouch.

6

GYMMIES
Established in 1961, Walsh has become one of Britain's specialist manufacturers of fell running shoes. Fondly remembered for providing 'gymmies' to the local school children of Bolton – this is a

The project focuses on refining the original brand ideas and spread the company's mission through various medias such as new business card, tag, CD package, and Edun post.

By tweaking the original logo and adding new secondary graphic: the triangle, the brand is more completed and tells a more compelling story and spirit.

CONSCIOUS & FAIR STYLE

EDUN IS FASHION BRAND CREATED WITH THE IDEA TO MAKE BEAUTIFUL CLOTHES IN A WAY THAT IS FAIR TO EVERYONE, AND IN A WAY THAT WOULD BENEFIT TO AFRICA

BONO AND ALI WENT TO AFRICA AND LIKE SO MANY OTHERS WERE MOVED BY THE PEOPLE AND THE LAND

THEY FOUNDED EDUN IN 2005 WITH THE COMMITMENT TO CREATE SUSTAINABLE TRADE AND PROMOTE LOCAL ECONOMIC OPPORTUNITIES IN AFRICA

AT EDUN WE STRIVE TO BE MORE THAN A FASHION BRAND. WE ARE DEDICATED TO CREATING A POSITIVE CHANGE IN THE WORLD

SALES	CREDITS
NORTH & SOUTH AMERICA	**PHOTOGRAPHER**
KARA COZZOLINO	
DOUGLAS MICHAEL	**STYLIST**
	MODEL
UNITED KINGDOM EUROPE, ASIA	**GROOMING**
KATE NEAL	**SHOES**
SABINA EBRAHIM	

PRESS CONTACT

VICKI REED

FW12 // MEN'S COLLECTION
EDUN.COM

FW12 ME
COLLECT

THE EDUN POST

CONSCIOUS & FAIR STYLE

edun.com

THE NEW LUXURY

WHAT IS EDUN? PAGE 2

EDUN IN AFRICA PAGE 4

VOI

IS GIVIN BACK

CONTENTS

LONG SLEEVE MULTI STRIPE
BUTTON DOWN SHIRT IN PEBBLE

ONE BUTTON MIXED WOOL
BLAZER IN CHARCOAL

SKINNY JEAN IN WAXED DENIM

FW12 // MEN'S COLLECTION
EDUN.COM

CONSCIOUS & FAIR STYLE

THE STORIES OF EDUN,
AND THE POSSIBILITY OF AFRICA

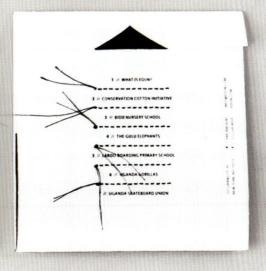

1 // WHAT IS EDUN?

2 // CONSERVATION COTTON INITIATIVE

3 // BIDII NURSERY SCHOOL

4 // THE GULU ELEPHANTS

5 // LABOU BOARDING PRIMARY SCHOOL

6 // UGANDA GORILLAS

// UGANDA SKATEBOARD UNION

FREIGAENGER
AGENCY: RAUM MANNHEIM
DESIGN: FRANK HOFFMANN
PHOTOGRAPHY: OPM FOTOGRAFIE
CLIENT: FREIGAENGER

Freigaenger is a small fashion label producing exclusive clothing.
Raum Mannheim developed a corporate identity, including
concepts for photography and advertising, and designed posters,
style-cards and a website for promotion.

KNOT

KNOT

TIMELESS

Knot is about creating longer and meaningful relationships with clothes through quality and design, to finding value beyond the ephemeral and momentary pleasure, and to shape your identity in strategic decisions while contributing to a less materialistic lifestyle.

The manner in which the garments will be identified will be with a cord, which refers to the timeline. When a costumer buys a garment, a knot will be made as a ritual, forming a timeless memory. The same way you tie a knot in your handkerchief to remember, the knot in the cord is a reminder of why you bought the garment.

KNOT

KNOT

10 Draycott Avenue, SW3 3AH, London
Tel: + 44 (0) 20 7823 1016 www.knot.com

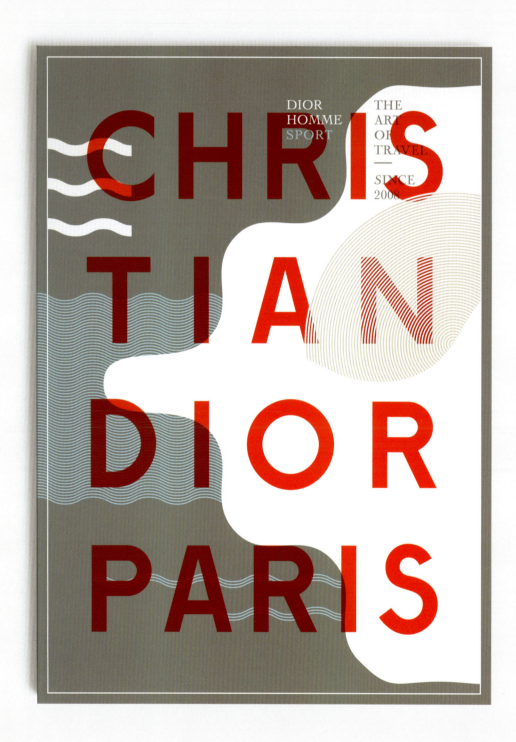

Design of cards for Dior Homme Sport.

Christian Dior quotes in posters.

Christian Dior

TISSU

MANNEQUIN

La robe et son mannequin sont souvent des éléments aussi inséparables que la robe et son tissu.

CHRISTIAN DIOR — LA ROBE ET SON MANNEQUIN SONT SOUVENT DES ÉLÉMENTS AUSSI INSÉPARABLES QUE LA ROBE ET SON TISSU.

Christian Dior

Même dans l'extra-vagance, la mode doit avoir du sens

La robe et son mannequin sont souvent des éléments aussi inséparables que la robe et son tissu.

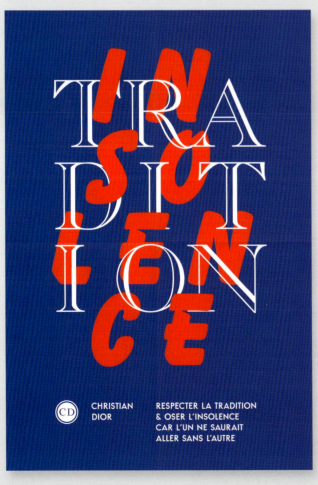

INSOLENCE
TRADITION

CHRISTIAN DIOR — RESPECTER LA TRADITION & OSER L'INSOLENCE CAR L'UN NE SAURAIT ALLER SANS L'AUTRE

CHRISTIAN DIOR — LA ROBE ET SON MANNEQUIN SONT SOUVENT DES ÉLÉMENTS AUSSI INSÉPARABLES QUE LA ROBE ET SON TISSU.

A COMPLETELY NEW LINE BY JULIAN RED
IN STORES AUGUST 15 TH 2011

WWW.JULIANJULIANJULIAN.COM

JULIAN RED is a Swedish clothing brand formed in 2003 by Mattias Lind. The name is taken from a character in Bret Easton Ellis' novel Less Than Zero. In the novel, Julian is misunderstood but he has a burning interest for art, music and literature. JULIAN RED also makes the JULIAN JULIAN JULIAN label, which is based on denim with a fine cut and comfortable material. Aoki produced the website, adverts and store materials.

FREDAG 18 MARS —— SÖNDAG 27 MARS

STYLA DIN EGEN LOOK I TOPSHOPS GODBITAR OCH POSERA
SEN I VÅRT FOTOBÅS OCH TA MED ETT MINNE HEM FRÅN DIN
UPPLEVELSE I DEN NYA TOPSHOP-BUTIKEN PÅ SERGELGATAN.
KOLLA IN VÅRT GALLERI OCH TAGGA DIG SJÄLV PÅ
WWW.FACEBOOK.COM/TOPSHOPSVERIGE

TOPSHOP

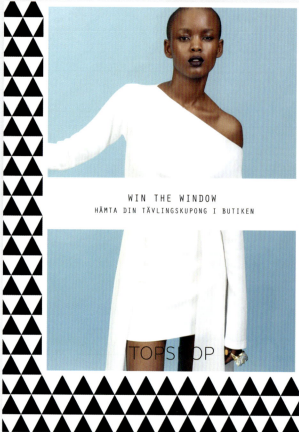

WIN THE WINDOW
HÄMTA DIN TÄVLINGSKUPONG I BUTIKEN

TOPSHOP

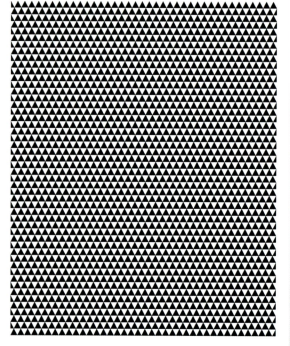

GRATTIS, DU HAR VUNNIT EN SHOPPINGUPPLEVELSE FÖR
5000KR I VÅR NYA TOPSHOP-BUTIK PÅ SERGELGATAN.
VISA UPP DETTA PRESENTKORT I KASSAN.
*INGA KONTANTER KAN GES I VÄXEL
*GILTIGT T.O.M. 31 MARS 2011

Marketing materials for Topshop store opening on Sergelgatan in Stockholm.
Flyers, Outdoor Advertising Invitations, Belly Bands, Tokens.

Marketing materials for Topshop Supports Fashion Targets
Breast Cancer. Flyers, instore materials, window design.

WITH EVERY
PURCHASE OF OUR
LIMITED EDITION
SLOGAN T-SHIRT £5.40
WILL BE DONATED TO
FASHION TARGETS
BREAST CANCER.

TO FIND OUT MORE,
VISIT TOPSHOP.COM/FTBC

MAKE
YOUR OWN
FASHION
STATEMENT
AND JOIN
TOPSHOP IN
SUPPORTING
FASHION
TARGETS
BREAST
CANCER
TOPSHOP

WITH EVERY
PURCHASE OF OUR
LIMITED EDITION
SLOGAN T-SHIRT
£5.40 WILL BE
DONATED TO
FASHION TARGETS
BREAST CANCER.

YOU CAN ALSO SHOW
YOUR SUPPORT BY
PURCHASING FASHION
TARGETS BREAST
CANCER MIRRORS AND
FRIENDSHIP BRACELETS
AT OUR TILL POINT.

SUSIE LAU
FASHION BLOGGER: STYLE BUBBLE

SUSIE LAU
FASHION BLOGGER: STYLE BUBBLE

TOPSHOP CHRISTMAS
DESIGN: JOHANNA BONNEVIER
ILLUSTRATION: ZOE MORE O'FERRALL

Christmas marketing campaign. Instore materials,
Consertina Flyers, Soup Van, Coups and Recipe Cards.

NATALIE CHRISTINE
DESIGN: MARTA PUCHALA

Natalie Christine is a London based, up and coming fashion and knitwear designer.

The brand aims to evoke the feminine, exclusive and confident attributes of her collections.

The interesting process and methodology inspired the circular patterns, illustration style, and wordmark. The logo has been designed to be light in weight and rounded in shape, like the thread joints in knitting.

The lookbook features an illustrated narrative about Natalie's journey to London. The illustrations were hand drawn with a thin pen to push the idea of lightness of thread. They work against the photography that provides a contrast. This idea is progressed through the various brand elements. Illustration against photography, matt off white paper against high gloss postcards, old materials against fresh designs.

Natalie
Christine

– Fashion & Knitwear –

– Diary of a Needle –

Winter 2010

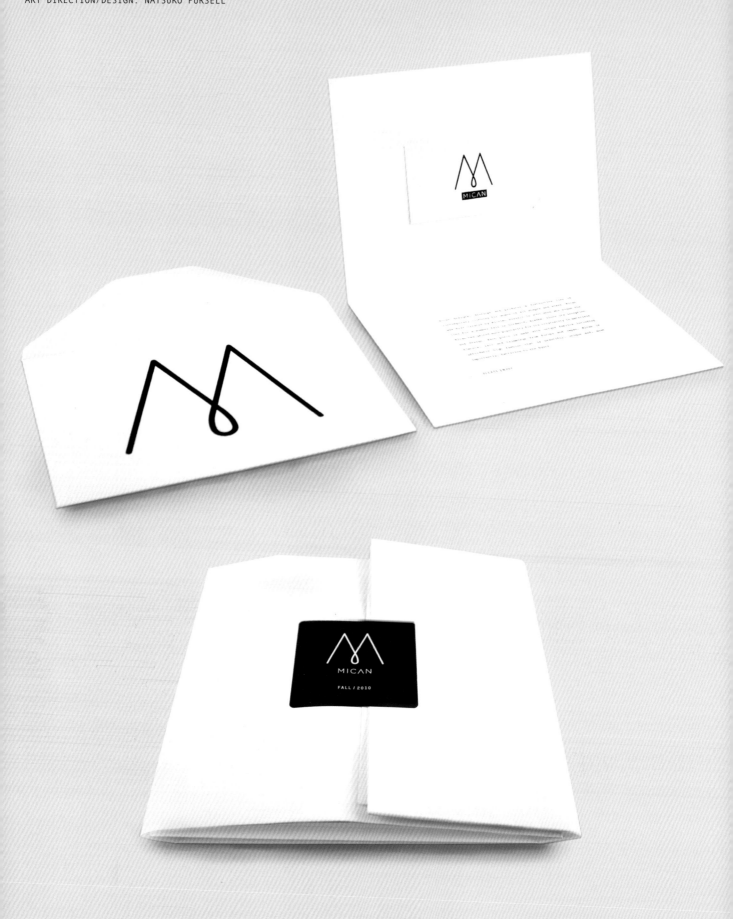

To launch a new clothing line, Natsuko used one small, insightful gesture to speak volumes about a brand. Taking inspiration from a simple sewn stitch, she expanded the 'M' shape into a logo, the Mican name itself, and entire visual identity of a company that reinterprets kimono fabrics and traditional materials into stunningly feminine designs. Combining that with surreal, sensual photography and elements of vertical Japanese type, she conveys the artisan attention to detail and unique synthesis of past and future that set the brand apart.

ly 20% of the
body. It sym
and commitr
scratched or
press creativ
soft graphite
also form the
natural mate
on earth as a
renowned fo

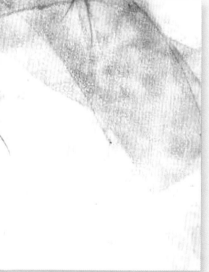

To create a visual identity for the new Chinese high-end men's fashion brand, "M-IDEA FOREVER", based on a strong concept, which expresses the brand's two fundamental characteristics; Avant Garde and Technology.

The Carbon Concept contains and supports the brand values and can, on several different levels of abstraction, be used as the DNA and source of inspiration for the creation and evolution of the whole identity.

Apart from the fact that the element Carbon forms the basis of all known life on Earth, it is exceptionally because of its diversity. Under different influences from its surroundings, Carbon can take various physical forms, each of which possess completely unique and diverse properties, although they are identical in their chemical composition. Looking at the raw graphite and polished diamond, it is fascinating to imagine that they are both composed of the element Carbon. Just like Carbon, the brand, M-IDEA FOREVER brand is characterised by its diversity. The new brand is based on a unique style composition, which mixes poetic Avant-Garde and functional Technology. Although very different, and sometimes even opposite, the two elements of M-IDEA FOREVER, tied together by the desire to constantly experiment, play together and strengthen each other. The black and soft Avant-Garde is expressed through the raw graphite. The bright and hard Technology grows out of the polished diamond. The Carbon Concept unites them.

NEW
CONCEPT
STORE
OPENING

M-IDEV FOREVER

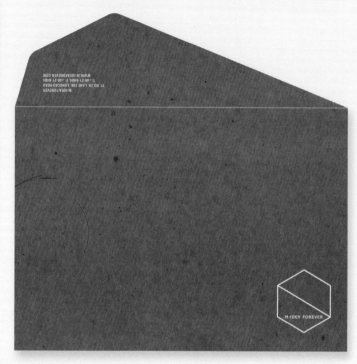

lab

NER RELOREM

amet, consectetuer adipiscing elit. In nibh arcu, aliquam pellentesque, orneu, malesuada
dolor sit amet psum dolor sit ame sit a.

venenatis faucibus turpis. Mauris vel nibh quis pede viverra eleifendrede. Maecenas luctus.
ac lectus. Phasellus ed massa eu arcu ornare gravidatn. Cras augue. Donec adipiscing
sse tincidunt adipiscing ipsum. Integer vel blandit massa vel asulla posuere est, eget
a ante. Integer lobortis diam av purus. Sed iaculis, li guendisse tempus venenatis sapien
en vel nibh mass.

lacinia non, euismod in, rhoncus sed, mi. Quisque eget augue et mauris feugiat euismod.
auris vitae quam. Nunc et magna. Fusce dapibus ultricies leo. Nulla posuere est, eget
s ante. Integer lobortis diam a purus. Sed iacu
endrerit, nisl velit cond dapibus hendrerit, ni.

vitae sapien. Pellentesque habitant morbi tristique senectus et netus et mal alesuada
s. Suspendisse arcu. In ipsum felis, consequat in, iaculis eu, rutrum sed, quam. Cras id
fringilla nisi. Aenea ida fringilla nisi.n.
re est, eget faucibus pede arcu quis ante. Integer lobortis diam a purused. Sed iaculis, li
rit, nisl velit condimentum orci, nec porttitor dui metus ind

lacinia non, euismod in, rhoncus sed, mi. Quisque eget augue et mauris feugiat euismod.
auris vitae quam. Nunc et magna. Fusce dapibus ultricies leo.nulla posuere est, eget
s ante. Integer lobortis diam a purus. Sed iacu
endrerit, nisl velit condimentum orci, nec porttito ger lobortis dia.

gna felis, elementum at, imperdiet id, pharetra eget, nunc. Aenean bland.
piscing varius lectus. Suspendisse tincidunt adipiscing ipsum. Integer vel blandit massa vel
t faucibus pede arcu quis ante. Integer lobortis diam av
Suspendiss.

M-IDEA FOREVER
7F, NO.28, LANE 208, LONGCAO ROAD
T: +86-21-6484. F: +86-21-6484
WWW.M-IDEAFOREVER.COM

Lorem ipsum dolor sit amet, consectetur adipiscing elit. Morbi eleifend dolor nec felis dapibus
fermentum. Suspendisse iaculis erat facilisis eros vulputate vehicula. Proin gravida viverra
ullamcorper. Cras imperdiet vulputate venenatis. Proin sit amet odio augue. Aliquam ultrices,
metus vitae posuere vestibulum, nibh lorem viverra sem, at sollicitudin ante nisl sed massa.
Vivamus arcu tellus, sollicitudin vitae elementum vitae, rutrum sed tortor. Nunc tristique
accumsan lacus, at rutrum turpis posuere accumsan. Nullam non enim purus. Proin volutpat
tellus lectus, id fringilla est. Proin non risus sed erat lobortis bibendum at at neque. Duis nec
dui dui. Sed dui nibh, rhoncus sit amet dignissim et, tempor sit amet

INVITATION

INVITATION

INVITATION

INVITATION

INVITATION

INVITATION

mj799-d
black /
cotton
au $127

August

01—09
2011

◆

3.

Danish
Anorak

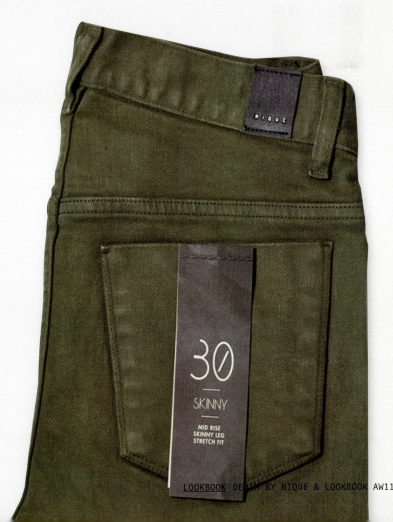

Studio SP-GD created a logo and collateral which still represented Nique yet also strayed from their conventional branding. In order to reflect a fresh new area signage was created for their st. kilda store.

Lookbook design and art direction for the Nique's AW11 Collection.

Fashion
g / Summer
-11

30

SKINNY

MID RISE
SKINNY LEG
STRETCH FIT

NIQUE

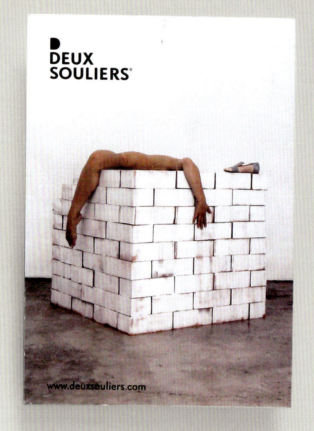

Deux Souliers is a footwear brand based in Barcelona.

A communication strategy, from art direction in photography, video, web and graphic design has been developed by Folch Studio. The product is presented as a still-life composition – as natural and pure as possible – resulting a contemporary and clean visual language.

Syndicate Original is a new Ukrainian brand, which was born on the tide of rising interest in traditional values. It was inspired by American heritage and American Indian culture, by Scandinavian simplicity and minimalism, by nautical and native themes. Clothing and accessories are produced in a workshop using traditional handicraft methods. Syndicate treats classic clothing designs in fresh and unique way. Orka Collective works in close collaboration with Syndicate from the very beginning. They share the same ideas and values. The collective developed the brand identity, the logotype and the website for Syndicate and also designed the first lookbook which was published in 2012 and several T-shirt collections.

Be Brave
Syndicate Exclusive by Orka Collective
100% fine cotton

grey melange

Syndicate Original
sailor's striped vest
100% cotton

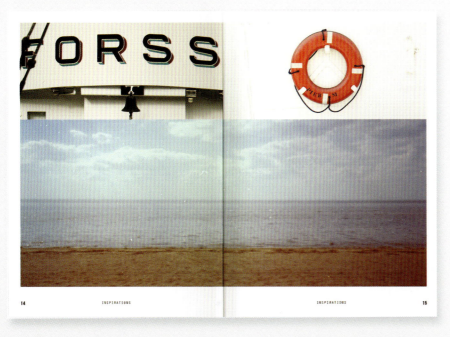

WupWup Fashion is an integral part of WupWup, a label and collective co-founded by Viktor Matic together with creative friends & artists from all around Europe. For the first WupWup fashion output Viktor designed a bag/bagpack and T-shirts with the slogan "tanzen ist auch sport". Together with Kamila Musilova he developed a lookbook and product pictures which are based on the WupWup and "tanzen ist auch sport" idea.

TANZEN IST AUCH SPORT.

WupWup

WUPWUP FASHION
»STORE.WUPWUP.COM«

LOOKBOOK BY KIKTOR&VAMILA
»WWW.KIKTOR-VAMILA.COM«

WITH BRAVE PARTICIPATION OF
JASMINE DEPORTA

INTRODUCTION BY
FATOŞ ERHUY

SEE, HEAR & FEEL MORE ON
»WWW.WUPWUP.COM«

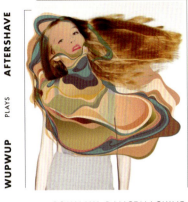

AFTERSHAVE

PLAYS

WUPWUP

SOUMAYA DANCEMACHINE
HIGH NEEDS LOW / BRUSSELS

+
WARM UP BY
XANDER&NIEDERREITER
www.wupwup.com

MICHAL ZIETARA
WUPWUP / SUXUL / MUNICH

FLOORIST
WUPWUP / MUNICH-BERLIN

TANZEN
IST AUCH
SPORT.

SAMSTAG

14·07·12

RENATE TANZEN IST AUCH SPORT

FAMILY AFFAIRS

15·09·12

DEEP DOWN DAVE & FLOORIST

TANZEN
IST AUCH
SPORT.

KO
NG

15·DEC·12
SHARON SCHAEL + OLIVER BARDUHN + DAVID GOLDBERG

TANZEN
IST AUCH
SPORT.

KO
NG

TIAS.001 RELEASE NIGHTS
12-05-2012 22H

XPEDIT VIENNA

Mr. Statik Lois Lane [live]
Flo Scheibein Nadipebi

TANZEN
IST AUCH
SPORT.

ÜBEL&GEFÄHRLICH

05
JAN
13
HAMBURG

TANZEN
IST AUCH
SPORT.

DYNAMODYSE
tias, we play house rec. cologne

TILMAN TAUSENDFREUND
hypercolour, dozier, contaminoising hamburg

MICHAL ZIETARA
tias, suxul munich-berlin

WupWup is a gathering of international artists
working in the fields of music, art, design, fashion
and event coordination. WupWup is co-founded
by Viktor Matic and works extensively in Bolzano-
Bozen, Berlin, Munich and Vienna.

floating bird china town
april 2012, new york

WupWup

"Floating Bird China Town" is the new WupWup
fashion lookbook featuring the 2012 "kurz&vogel"
T-shirt collection by Viktor Matic. The lookbook is
made in collaboration with the photographers Monica
Lek & Jasmine Deporta – New York, April 2012.

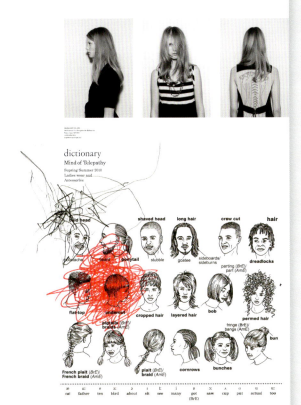

Rikako Nagashima was commissioned to design the catalog for fashion brand dictionary's spring and summer collection. Due to "dictionary" being the brand's name, Rikako Nagashima's concept for the catalog design was to imitate a genuine dictionary. She set the layout with some dictionary-like illustrations, along with some words and expressions associated with textiles and styling. Hereby, the dictionary-like catalog visually interprets the brand itself well.

TELEGRAM /ˈteləˌɡræm/ n [U] a message sent by telegraph

TELEGRAPH /ˈteləˌɡrɑːf/ n [U] an old fashioned WAY OF sending MESSAGES using electrical SIGNALS

TELEPATHY /təˈlepəθi/ n the ability to communicate thoughts DIRECTLY to someone else's mind with out SPEAKING or writing

TELEPHONE /ˈteləˌfəʊn/ also phone n [C] a piece of equipment you USE to SPEAK to someone who is in another PLACE

T-SHIRTS 16800 yen
long sailor pants 94,500 yen
straw hat 32,000 yen
stripe necklace 24,100 yen

BORDER HAREM SUIT 28,400 yen

BEADS NECKLACE 39,450 yen

VINTAGE WASH COAT DRESS 48,300 yen
HAIR BAND 13,650 yen

dictionary
Mind of Telepathy

Spring-Summer 2010
Ladies wear and Accessories

MOSSLIGHT CO.,LTD

NIKE: JOURNEY TO GREATNESS

DESIGN/DIRECTION: JOE JOINER, ALISTAIR HANSON, CRESSIDA O'MAHONY AND ROB WILSON

"Confront, Persist, Succeed" CCW
T-shirt commission.

The aim was to evoke certain
aspects and emotions of an athlete's
journey, without being too literal.
The powerful, industrial form of the
mangle representing the pressure of
the moment, combined with the fragile
yet malleable strength of the balloon
that signified the fine line between
failure and success.

Inspired by the ECHELON typeface, Samuel Mensah was compelled to make a series of garment with a message that was prominent to him at the time. The message of Youth and its prevalence in life. They say youth is wasted on the young. When you look at it the youth are who they are because they're young. Value your youth, live young. Make mistakes and learn from them. Our creativity comes from our youth and the beauty of living young is that it has nothing to do with age. Don't grow up it's a trap.

YOUNG
& NUMB

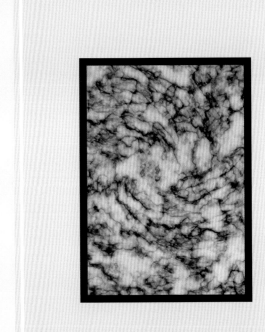

FUTURE
ICONS

DIANA ORVING

LIGHT
autumn/winter 2010

Tisdag 2 februari
Berns, Stora salongen
Insläpp 14.00, visning 14.30

OSA: dianaorving@jus.se
senast 29 januari

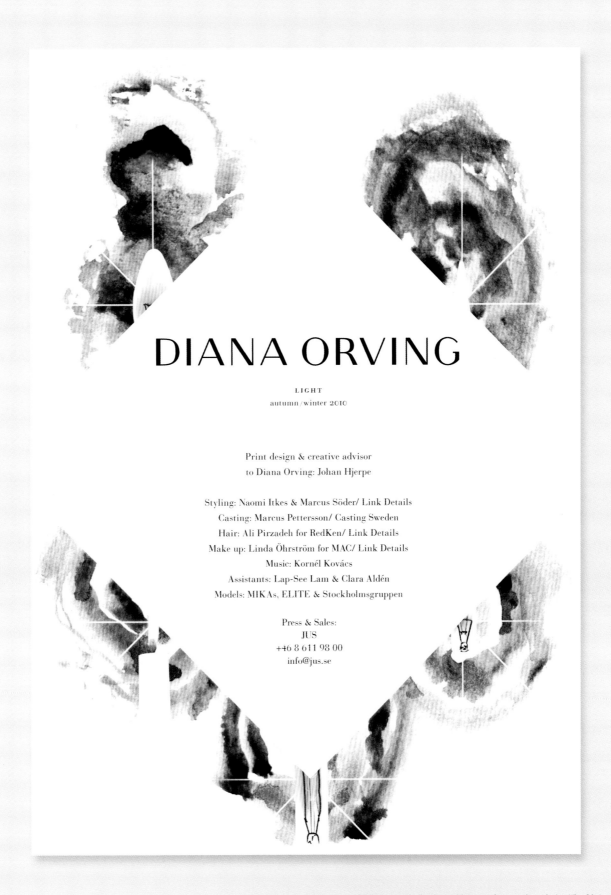

DIANA ORVING

LIGHT
autumn / winter 2010

Print design & creative advisor
to Diana Orving: Johan Hjerpe

Styling: Naomi Itkes & Marcus Söder/ Link Details
Casting: Marcus Pettersson/ Casting Sweden
Hair: Ali Pirzadeh for RedKen/ Link Details
Make up: Linda Öhrström for MAC/ Link Details
Music: Kornél Kovács
Assistants: Lap-See Lam & Clara Aldén
Models: MIKAs, ELITE & Stockholmsgruppen

Press & Sales:
JUS
+46 8 611 98 00
info@jus.se

Bright autumn bulbs shine with inverted watercolour glorias. The fabric print
design is also used as graphics for printed matter such as the invitation and
information sheet you see here.

DIANA ORVING AW11 "YOU"

ART DIRECTION/PRINT DESIGN: JOHAN HJERPE
PHOTOGRAPHY: MARCUS PALMQVIST
STYLING: TEKLA KNAUST
MODEL: SARA ASSBRING (ARTIST EL PERRO DEL MAR)

CAPE No; 1184
STRAP DRESS No; 1160

TORSO COAT No; 1183
KNITTED LACE SKIRT No; 1144

KNITTED TOP No; 1140
TWISTED SKIRT No; 1178

SHAPE DRESS No; 1155
HALF MOON SCARF No; 1107

DRAPED JACKET No; 1181
CURVE TROUSERS No; 1168

BLOCK T-SHIRT N0¡ 1153
TWISTED SKIRT N0¡ 1178

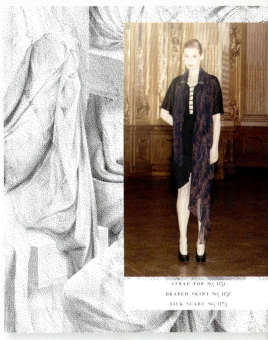

STRAP TOP N0¡ 1151
DRAPED SKIRT N0¡ 1156
SILK SCARF N0¡ 1173

Marble statues from the collection of the Louvre is reduced to drapings and paired with a marble texture pattern. Final artworks for the textile prints are also applied directly to the look book paper, adding a rough contrast to the grandiose environments.

LONG COAT N0¡ 1182
LONG SHIRT N0¡ 1171
CURVE TROUSERS N0¡ 1168

SHORT BLOUSE N0¡ 1166
CURVE TROUSERS N0¡ 1168

DIANA ORV

YOU
autumn winter 2011

DIANA ORVING SS08 "I, I, I"
ART DIRECTION/PRINT DESIGN: JOHAN HJERPE
FASHION PHOTOGRAPHY: ERIK WÄHLSTRÖM
STYLING: STINA PERSSON-HELLEDAY

The collection I, I, I is designed through interlacing three different temperaments within the same personality. The three dimensions is explored in variations of poses and expressions in the look book. The textile print design exposes variations of a persona with totem-like draped figurines.

AUTOMNE

D (&) J **TU** AMOS FRICKE

M'AS VOLÉ L'ÉTÉ

REDONNE—LE MOI

IL ME MANQUE TELLEMENT.

DEUTSCHE & JAPANER AVEC

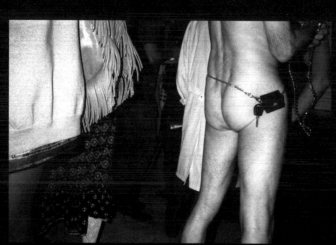

A F

AF / OI-01
OUTLOOKS INSIGHTS

12

Fall is a thief. He stole the summer. DEUTSCHE & JAPANER is craving to get it back. The T-shirt "Automne" is a collaborative project together with Amos Fricke, a photographer working in fashion, portrait and still life based in Berlin. It's a declaration of love to the European summer months.

DEVOA AW09/10 COLLECTION INVITATION

AGENCY: NIGN COMPANY LIMITED
DESIGN: KENICHIRO OHARA

DEVOA is a Japanese fashion brand, initiated by Daiske Nishida, a designer with a unique background of sports physiology. To integrate his background on the collection, 2009-2010 AW collection's theme was set as "materiality and stereoscopic". The invitation card took in the essences of the theme with a solidity of the invitation's form, which was initially shrink-wrapped.

The wrapping process was done manually and each card was rolled and packed in a way that gold parts, which happens to be the typeface, emerges on the front. Once the package is opened and the card is spread, its organic texture reminds of the body parts - an essence of physiology.

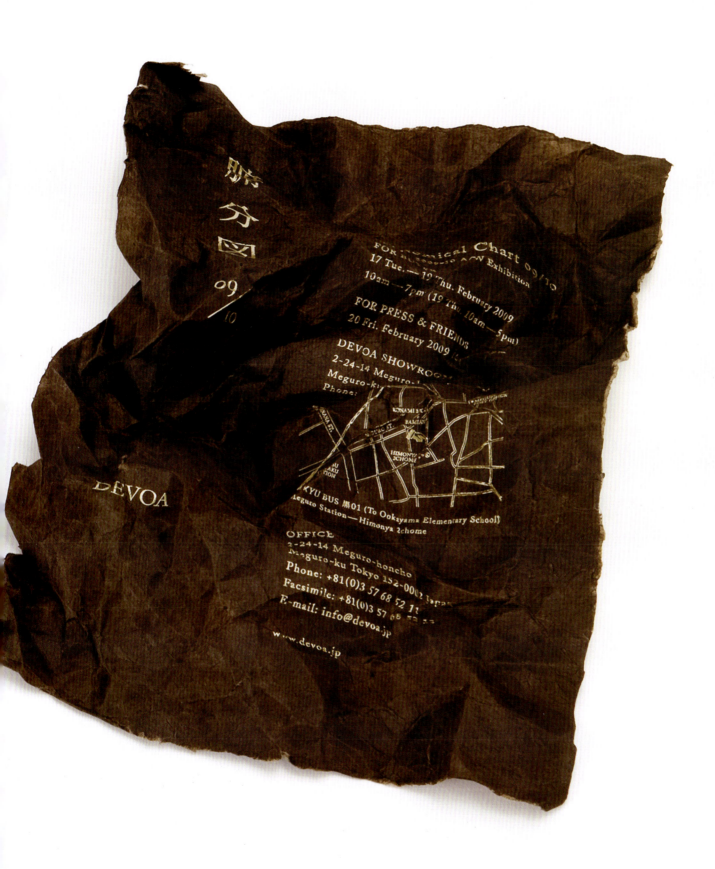

THE VIRIDI-ANNE SS12 COLLECTION INVITATION
AGENCY: NIGN COMPANY LIMITED
DESIGN: KENICHIRO OHARA

The Viridi-anne is a fashion brand, initiated and produced by Tomoaki Okaniwa. The brand holds two collections in Paris every year and 2012 Spring/Summer Collection's theme was "incomplete". The invitation card expressed the theme with totally incomplete expression - an invitation card is folded unevenly and all the characters were handwritten. The typography on the back also reflects the concept of incompleteness.

THE VIRIDI-ANNE AW09/10 COLLECTION INVITATION

AGENCY: NIGN COMPANY LIMITED
DESIGN: KENICHIRO OHARA

THE VIRIDI-ANNE
2009-10 AUTUMN & WINTER COLLECTION
"CHRYSALIS"

FOR BUYER 18TH - 19TH FEBRUARY 11:00 - 19:00
(APPOINTMENT REQUIRED)

FOR PRESS & FRIENDS 20TH FEBRUARY 12:00 - 19:00

AT SPACE EDGE (SPACE A)
3-26-7 SHIBUYA SHIBUYA-KU
TOKYO 150-0002 JAPAN

BY AIRMAIL

POST OFFICE
JAPAN
POSTAGE
PAID

INVITATION

The Viridi-anne is a fashion brand, initiated and produced by Tomoaki Okaniwa. The brand holds two collections in Paris every year and 2009-2010 Autumn/Winter Collection's theme was "chrysalis". The invitation card incorporated essences of the theme with its form and material. Three-layered thin envelopes, treated with wax and crease finish, were employed to create a sense of solidity. A black card, with a hologram stamp of an insect, was inserted in the envelope to visually express chrysalis.

THE VIRIDI-ANNE SS11 COLLECTION INVITATION
AGENCY: NIGN COMPANY LIMITED
DESIGN: KENICHIRO OHARA

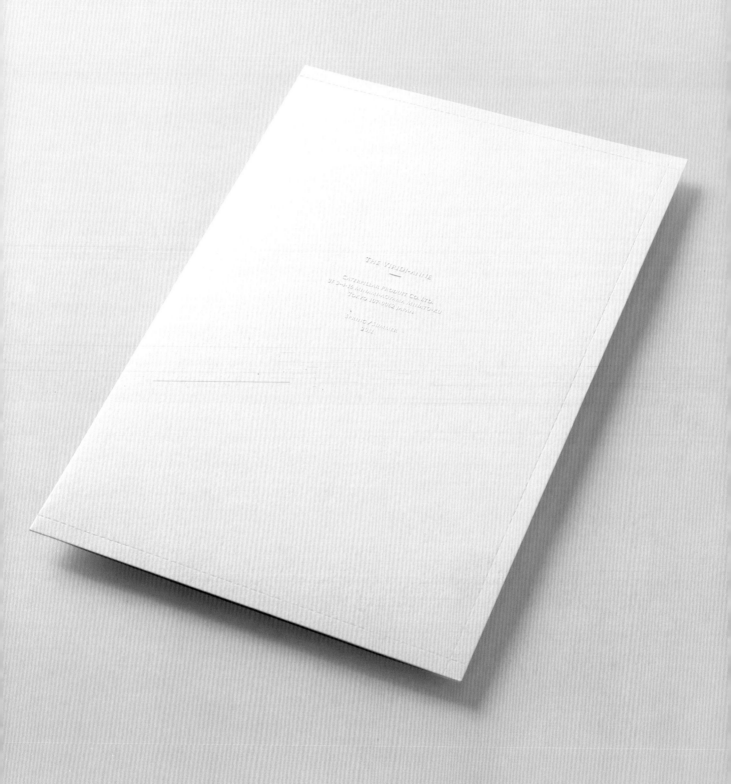

THE VIRIDI-ANNE

CATERPILLAR PRODUIT CO.,LTD.
3F 3-4-16 MINAMI-AOYAMA, MINATO-KU
TOKYO 107-0062 JAPAN

SPRING/SUMMER
2011

The Viridi-anne is a fashion brand, initiated and produced by Tomoaki Okaniwa. The brand holds two collections in Paris every year and 2011 Spring/ Summer Collection's theme was "blue period". The invitation card expressed the theme by allocating "moment" between a white card and thin blue paper.

P / E 2012

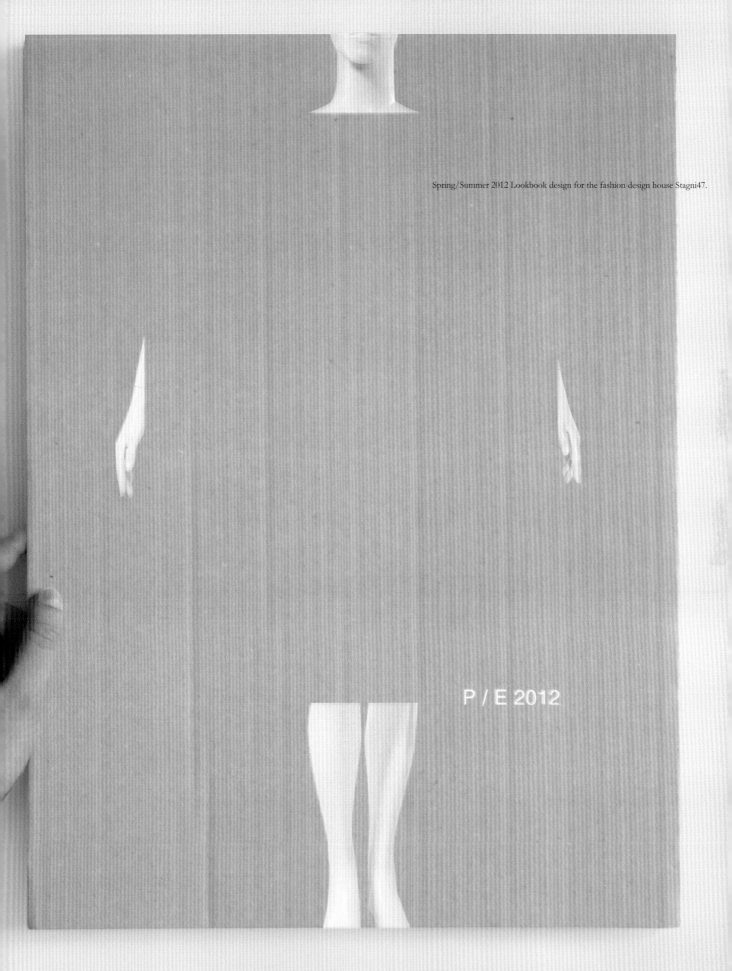

Spring/Summer 2012 Lookbook design for the fashion design house Stagni47.

P / E 2012

Invitation designed for Day Dream Nation Autumn/Winter 2008.

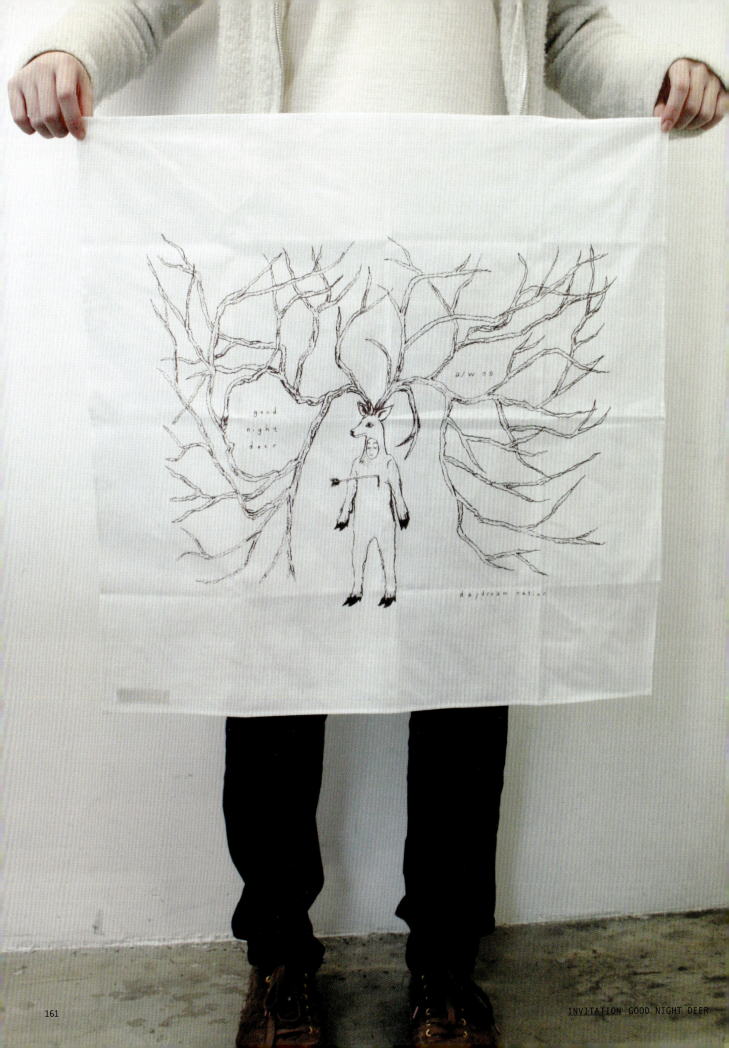

Fall/Winter 2010-2011 Lookbook design for the fashion design house Stagni47.

Francesca Cremonesi collection
is made using the technique of
moulage - the art of draping
on the body. This tailoring is to
model the fabric directly on the
mannequin to create volumes in
perfect harmony with the body.

The logo is a signature freehand
highlighting the craftsmanship.The
card is made with paper to paper
model used in sewing, the folds
evoke the technique of moulage
and on the back is the explanation
of the technique.

The background of the website
consists of folds of paper, and
recall the technique is different
from section to section.

Il Moulage nasce in Francia negli anni '20 come arte del drappeggio sul corpo.
È una tecnica sartoriale che consiste nel modellare il tessuto direttamente sul manichino
fino alla creazione di volumi in perfetta armonia con il corpo.
Durante il processo creativo tutto può essere modificato, rimodellato, ricostruito
per giungere ad un progetto architettonico nel quale tutto è immediatamente visib

READ
ME
BEFORE
WEAR

i am the in
part of wom
sexy + soft
i have my
natural bea
i am also
affected by
traditional
chinese cult
my body have
been inherite
imprint from
time and sun
light.

READ
ME
BEFORE
WEAR

i am the inner
part of women:
sexy + soft.
i have my
natural beauty.
i am also
affected by
traditional
chinese cultur
my body have
been inherite
imprint from
time and sun
light.

READ
ME
BEFORE
WEAR

i am the inner
part of women:
sexy + soft.
i have my
natural beauty.
i am also
affected by
traditional
chinese culture.
my body have
been inherited
imprint from the
time and sun
light.

R
M
B
W

i
pa
s
i
n
i
a

The concept of doing a collection is to carry some message to communicate and to share with others.

Missman is a collection that sharing about new style of women: they have strong characteristic but still trapped by the lock of traditional Chinese culture. Now, women are in progress to establish their new style. Missman is reflecting this contradiction and instable status.

LOUIS VUITTON ORIGAMI
PROJECT BY: HAPPYCENTRO
PROJECT MANAGER: FEDERICO PADOVANI
PAPER OBJECT DESIGN: FEDERICO GALVANI
INSTRUCTION SHEET ILLUSTRATION: ANDREA MANZATI
PHOTO RETOUCHING: MARCO "OIO" OLIOSI
PRINT MANAGEMENT: RICCARDO ZAMBELLI AND BARBARA BONI @
STUDIO FASOLI FOR MANAGING ALL PRODUCTION STEPS
GRAPHICART (MICHELE ADAMI) FOR OFFSET PRINTING
TIPOGRAFIA ECONOMICA (RICKY E MATTIA PATTARO) FOR DRY DEBOSSING
EUROIMMAGINE (GIULIO ZANGRANDI, FRANCESCA E FEDERICO) FOR SILK PRINTING
LA CARTOTECNICA (FABRIZIO SONA) FOR DIE CUTTING

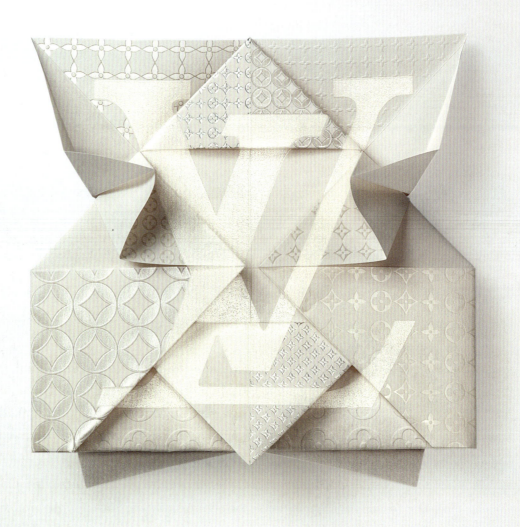

INVITATION LOUIS VUITTON ORIGAMI

What Happycentro did was radical because of its whispering nature. Slow, silent, careful, precise gestures, a sequence of microns over a thin paper sheet, foils, inks, reliefs on top or beside of each other, tone over tone, to give a welcome, in the era of outputs and special fx, this is theirs.

AGENCY: ROANDCO
CREATIVE DIRECTION: ROANNE ADAMS
DESIGN: TADEU MAGALHÃES
PHOTOGRAPHY: KT AULETA

Honor, a high-end women's luxury brand, wanted to create something unique and luxurious for the launch of their brand. RoAndCo pulled inspiration from 1960's French films, Le Ballon Rouge and Belle Du Jour, to help establish Honor's collection image. Inspired by all things Parisian, the show invitation came in a box along with gourmet macarons, which created a buzz in the fashion community and a large turnout at the show.

BE NOISY
CREATIVE DIRECTION: RIKAKO NAGASHIMA
ART DIRECTION: RIKAKO NAGASHIMA
DESIGN: RIKAKO NAGASHIMA, NAONORI YAGO,
NAOKO MAEDA, YURI KIMOTO
PHOTOGRAPHY: YASUTOMO EBISU
HAIR STYLE: KATSUYA KAMO

be noisy. LAFORET

Harajuku is the place where a large number of young people get together. In the old days we could find young people dressed in unusual clothes; however it is getting rare to see young people dress like "Harijuku fashion", a fashion full of energy these days. They seem to be subdued, as Japanese fashion designers. However, the future is in hands of young ones. When we encourage people to create the new world, we do need "noisy unidentified energy" and "noisy life force". So Laforet Harajuku gave a message "be noisy" to the young generation of Harajuku, and expressed "unidentified energy" and "life force". Rikako Nagashima applied multicolor to the advertisement of Laforet Harajuku spring and summer collection, as well as black and white to autumn and winter collection so as to embody the feeling of each season.

be noisy. LAFORET

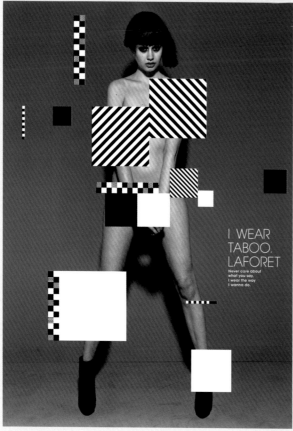

This is the corporate advertising of Laforet Harajuku, a commercial complex in the center of Japanese fashion culture. In the world of rapidly changing fashion, young people who wear personalized clothing are reducing in Harajuku. Everyone seems to be pursuing the same fashion trend. However, being different is also another embodiment of fashion. While delivering the message of "I wear taboo" to the young ladies, the spirit of Laforet Harajuku and the essence of something called fashion get manifested. Rikako Nagashima applied multicolor to the advertising materials of the Laforet Harajuku spring and summer collection, as well as black and white to autumn and winter collection so as to embody the feeling of each season.

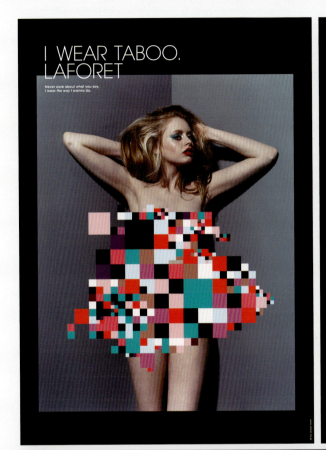

MONKI CAMPAIGN - MIRROR MOVEMENT

PRODUCER/FASHION DIRECTOR: EMMA WICKSTRÖM/ENTOURAGE
DESIGN: MONKI
PHOTOGRAPHY: AORTA/LUNDLUND

Emma Wickström created a photo concept for the chain Monki. They wanted something different with a strong DNA. So she created a graphic surreal world for the costumers and the Monki fans.

MONKI CAMPAIGN - WILD AND TAME

PRODUCER/FASHION DIRECTOR: EMMA WICKSTRÖM/ENTOURAGE
DESIGN: MONKI
PHOTOGRAPHY: AORTA/LUNDLUND

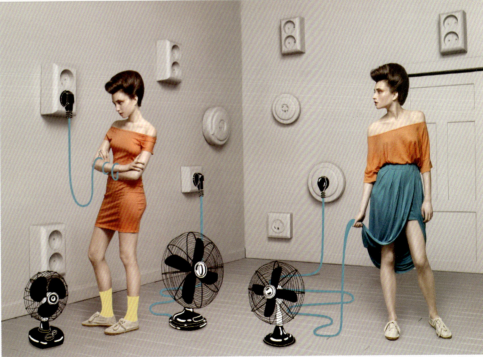

Emma Wickström created a photo concept for the chain Monki. They wanted something different with a strong DNA. So she created a graphic surreal world for the costumers and the Monki fans.

MONKI CAMPAIGN - EXPLORING WONDERLAND

PRODUCER/FASHION DIRECTOR: EMMA WICKSTRÖM/ENTOURAGE
DESIGN: MONKI
PHOTOGRAPHY: AORTA/LUNDLUND

Emma Wickström created a photo concept for the chain Monki. They wanted something different with a strong DNA. So she created a graphic surreal world for the costumers and the Monki fans.

MONKI CAMPAIGN - IN A SECRET GARDEN

PRODUCER/FASHION DIRECTOR: EMMA WICKSTRÖM/ENTOURAGE
DESIGN: MONKI
PHOTOGRAPHY: AORTA/LUNDLUND

Emma Wickström created a photo concept for the chain Monki. They wanted something different with a strong DNA. So she created a graphic surreal world for the costumers and the Monki fans.

MONKI CAMPAIGN - SWEET REBELS

PRODUCER/FASHION DIRECTOR: EMMA WICKSTRÖM/ENTOURAGE
DESIGN: MONKI
PHOTOGRAPHY: AORTA

Emma Wickström created a photo concept for the chain Monki. They wanted something different with a strong DNA. So she created a graphic surreal world for the costumers and the Monki fans.

M4 Models asked Eps51 to design sedcards for Bread and Butter 2012. Instead of just a photograph on the front they created eye-catching pattern-illustrations.

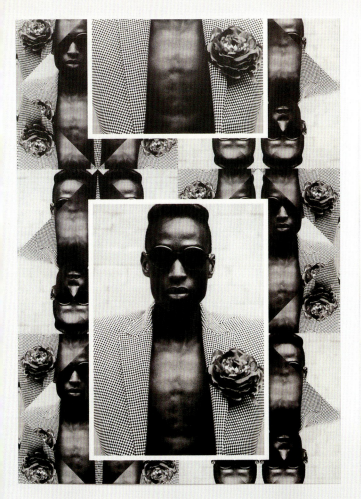

BERLIN@M4MODELS.DE
WWW.M4MODELS.DE

M4 MODELS GMBH
T +49 30 616606-6

M4
Philipp Lukié

GRÖSSE 185 OBERWEITE 81	HEIGHT 6´1˝ BUST 32
TAILLE 67 HÜFTE 86	WAIST 26.5 HIPS 33.5
SCHUHE 42 HAARE SCHWARZ	SHOES 9 US HAIR BLACK
AUGEN BRAUN	EYES BROWN

BERLIN@M4MODELS.DE
WWW.M4MODELS.DE

M4 MODELS GMBH
T +49 30 616606-6

M4
Charlotte

GRÖSSE 180 OBERWEITE 80	HEIGHT 5´11˝ BUST 32
TAILLE 60 HÜFTE 89	WAIST 24 HIPS 35
SCHUHE 41 HAARE BLOND	SHOES 9.5 US HAIR BLONDE
AUGEN GRÜN	EYES GREEN

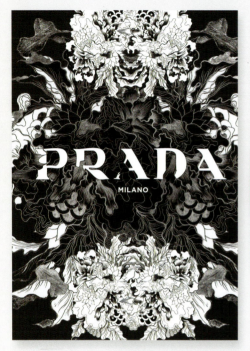

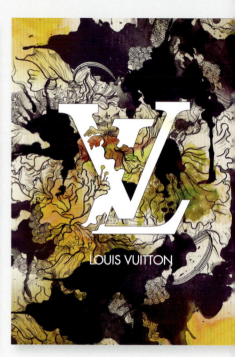

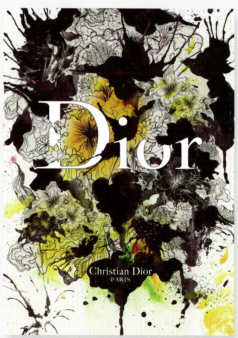

Brands in Full Bloom is a self-promotion project that features 6 famous designer brands illustrated in a feminine and organic mood adorned with lavishing flaura theme and blowing watercolors while still retaining each of the brands' sophistication and identity.

The project shows the illustrator's new-found personal style combining floral themes of rough hand-drawn sketches and blowing watercolors, composed and polished digitally.

Brands include Dior, Chanel, Alexander McQueen, Saint Laurent, Prada and Louis Vuitton.

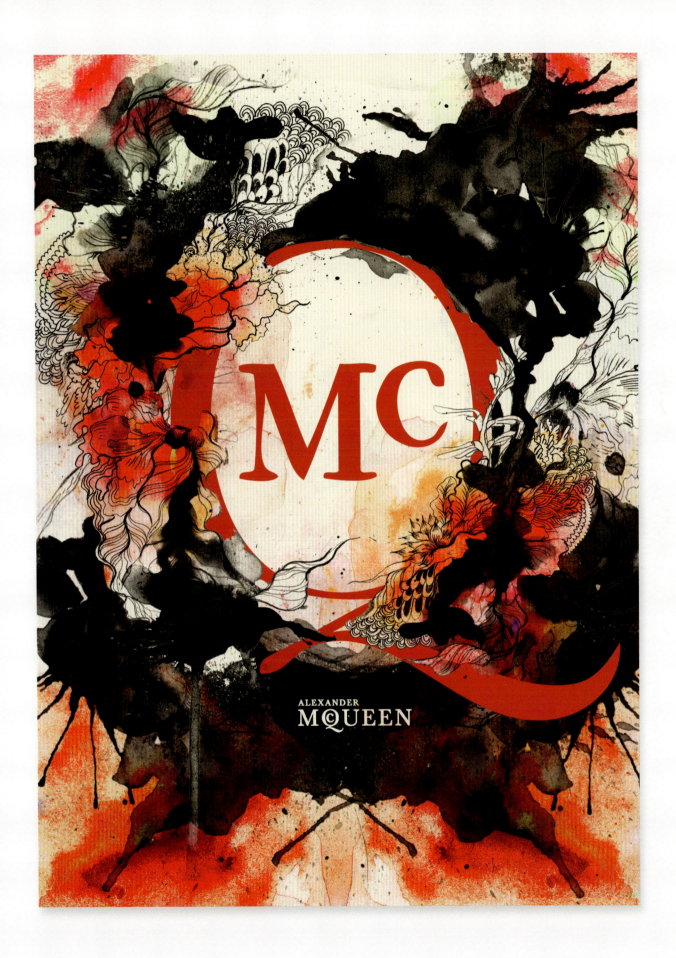

LONG LEGGED PETS / HIGH SHOULDERS
AGENCY: LIVINGROOM COMMUNICATION, UAE
CREATIVE DIRECTION: MARTINO O'BRIEN, MANSOOR A. BHATTI
ART DIRECTION: JANA JELOVAC, LARA BIZRI, NISREEN
SHAHIN, MANSOOR A. BHATTI
COPYWRITER: SARAH BERRO
ILLUSTRATION: JANA JELOVAC

Lady Fozaza's jackets come with the signature "High Shoulders".
The advertising shows the effect of these high shoulders on the
shoulder pets.

FACTORY FOX

Factory Fox is a young fashion designer duo from The Hague. Together they create a wide variety of items such as T-shirts, sweats, lingerie, jewelry and other accessory. Also they run a blog about fashion, events and traveling.

The identity had to be objective towards the different seasons and trends in their brand. Therefore it is all in black and white to give the idea of packaging, to wrap around the different projects and to be easy editable.

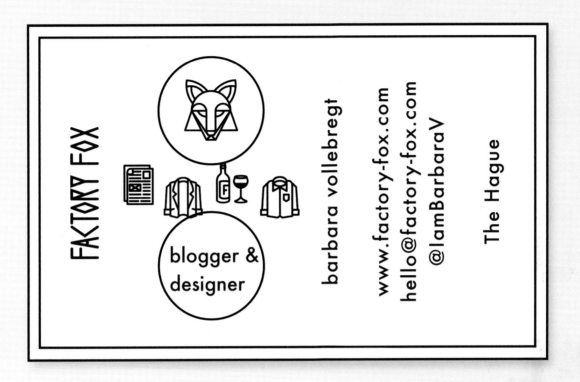

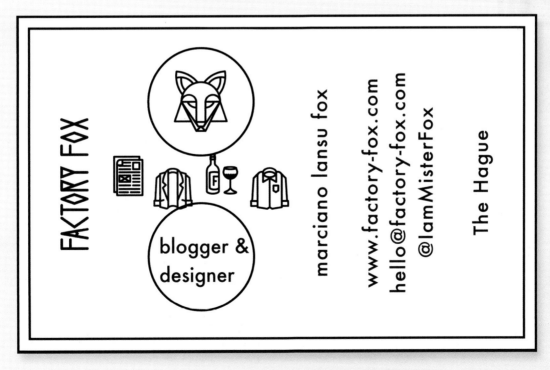

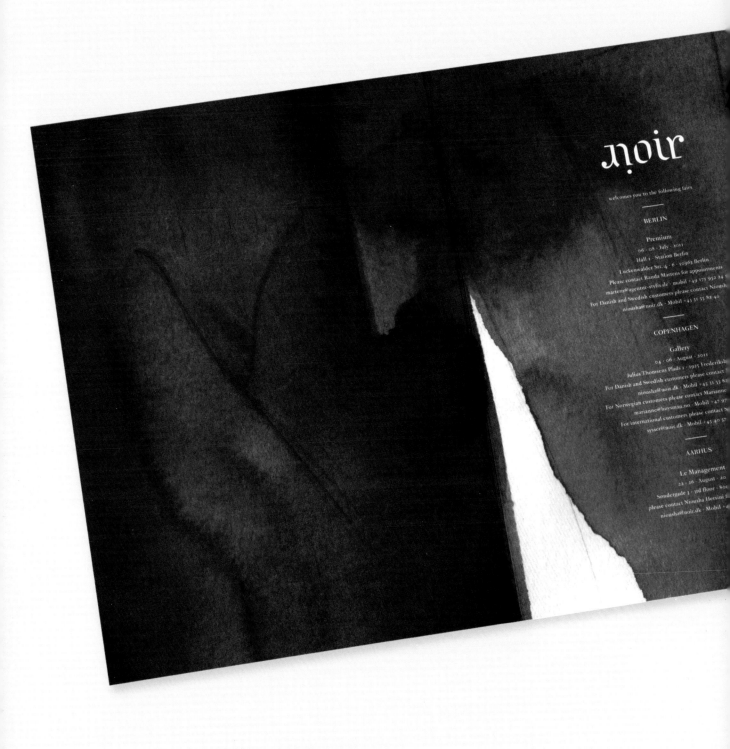

Spring/Summer 2011 invitation designed for Noir.

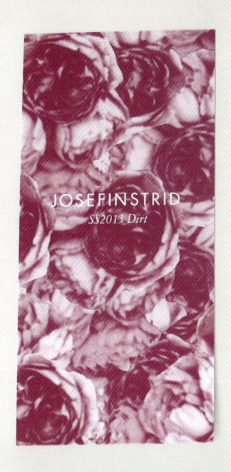

JOSEFINSTRID
SS2013 Dirt

Mark, invitation and thank you card designed and produced for the SS13 show taking place during Stockholm Fashion Week at Berns. Hi-fashion inspired from street style culture, using patterns and graphics from the hip-hop world.

BOYZ SHIRT
YONKER
KICK VEST
SKANK BLAZER
AT SHIRT
FINK BLAZER
DOLLAR JACKET
EXPLICIT
FATTY TANK
BOOM TANK
O TANK
ROCKY JACKET
STARR TROUSER
1991

JOSEFINSTRID
SS2013 Dirt

TACK TILL
TILLVAXTVERKET, GILETTE, ONITSUKA TIGER, HAIRCARE BY MARC ANTHONY, HAPPY PLUGS, PRETTO PR, TEREZA ORTIZ, DALSTON CREATIVE, RAGNAR BERN MED TEAM, JOSEFIN SCHERDIN MED TEAM/MIKAS LOOKS, KALLE EKLUND MED TEAM/MIKAS LOOKS, SANDRA SILJESTEDT, OSKAR LANDSTROM, JOHANNA BOLANDER, NISCH MANAGEMENT, MIKAS, ELITE MODELS, STOCKHOLMSGRUPPEN, BUTONIA MODEINKUBATORN, MARKETPLACE BORÅS

Invitation sent out to guests of the Spring/ Summer 2011 collection. The invitation included a card that opened to reveal a pop-up 3D box that had to have the seal cut open by the guest. Inside the box was a small invitation card/ ticket and a special gift of a pressed flower in a small stand-up frame.

Several of the pieces in the collection included hundreds of overlapping chiffon flower petals, a device that was referenced throughout the mailers and marketing materials.

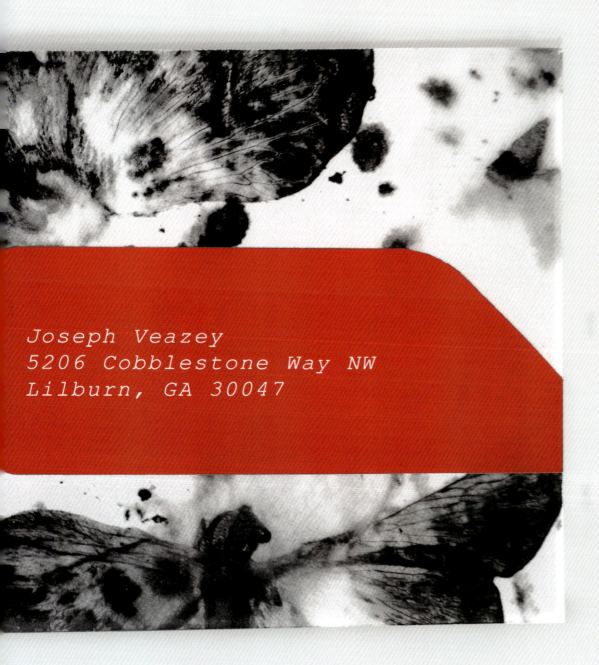

Joseph Veazey
5206 Cobblestone Way NW
Lilburn, GA 30047

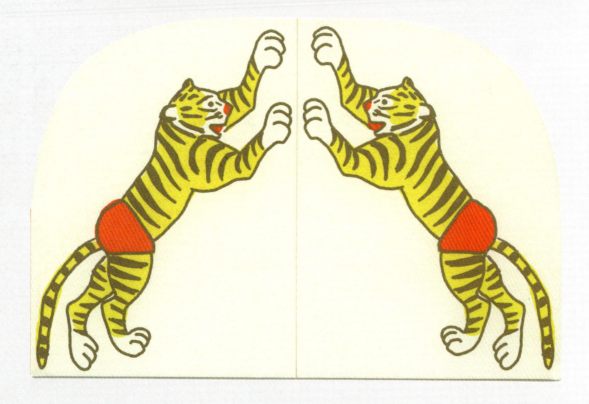

mercibeaucoup,

はじめまして。　どうぞよろしく。

It comes from the bland theme "thank you very much" and "nice to see you" because it is the first collection of Mercibeaucoup.

mercibe

はじめまして。

Stationery and Business Cards for F-troupe.
British celebrities, landmarks, and clichés
were incorporated into the brand vocabulary
to portray the unconventional, sarcastic,
"quintessentially British" personality of F-troupe
and its shoes.

ASOS SS13 CAMPAIGN
ART DIRECTION: PATRICK WAUGH
DESIGN: CASPER CHAN
PRODUCTION: ASOS CREATIVE

ASOS.com is a global online fashion and beauty retailer and offers on the ASOS.com website over 50,000 branded and own label product lines across womenswear, menswear, footwear, accessories, jewellery and beauty. ASOS has websites targeting the UK, USA, France, Germany, Spain, Italy and Australia and also ships to over 190 other countries from its central distribution centre in the UK.

To celebrate the diversity in style, ASOS SS/13 branding and identity echoes this concept with a refreshing visual identity ranging from print invitation, image disc, press release, digital website to bespoke iPad lookbook.

Identity design for Converse Nights; four nights of music in the Netherlands and Belgium. The design is a mixture of sprays, drips and the Chuck Taylor sole pattern.

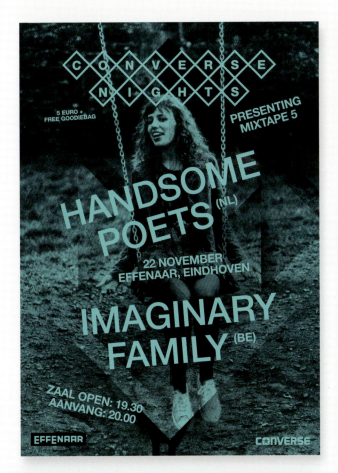

CONVERSE NIGHTS

5 EURO +
FREE GOODIEBAG

PRESENTING
MIXTAPE 5

HANDSOME POETS (NL)

22 NOVEMBER
EFFENAAR, EINDHOVEN

IMAGINARY FAMILY (BE)

ZAAL OPEN: 19.30
AANVANG: 20.00

EFFENAAR

CONVERSE

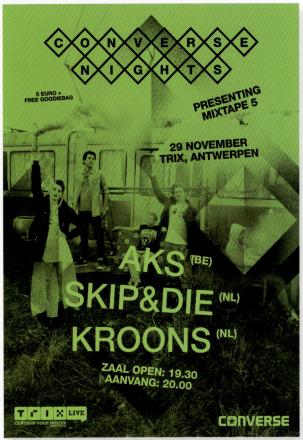

CONVERSE NIGHTS

5 EURO +
FREE GOODIEBAG

PRESENTING
MIXTAPE 5

29 NOVEMBER
TRIX, ANTWERPEN

AKS (BE)
SKIP&DIE (NL)
KROONS (NL)

ZAAL OPEN: 19.30
AANVANG: 20.00

TRIX LIVE
CENTRUM VOOR MUZIEK

CONVERSE

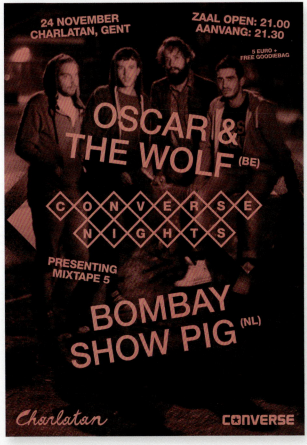

24 NOVEMBER
CHARLATAN, GENT

ZAAL OPEN: 21.00
AANVANG: 21.30

5 EURO +
FREE GOODIEBAG

OSCAR & THE WOLF (BE)

CONVERSE NIGHTS

PRESENTING
MIXTAPE 5

BOMBAY SHOW PIG (NL)

Charlatan

CONVERSE

CONVERSE NIGHTS

PRESENTING
MIXTAPE 5

5 EURO +
FREE GOODIEBAG

DRIVE LIKE MARIA (NL)

8 DECEMBER
TIVOLI DE HELLING, UTRECHT

DRUMS ARE FOR PARADES (BE)

ZAAL OPEN: 19.30
AANVANG: 20.15

TIVOLI
DE HELLING

CONVERSE

1. Drive Like Maria—Where The Brokenhearted Go
   (Drive Like Maria) ZooStudios/PIAS, 2012
2. Kensington—It Doesn't Have To Hurt
   (Vultures) Universal, 2012
3. Bombay Show Pig—Sancho Panza
   (Vulture/Provider) Kytopia, 2012
4. Daily Bread—Loverst
   (ITERUM) Excelsior, 2012
5. Handsome Poets—Sky On Fire
   (Single) Handsome Poets, 2012
6. Imaginary Family—The Bird Watcher
   (Single) Unday, 2012
7. AKS—Round & Round
   (Out Of Control) Waste Your Weekend/
   Beatz & Bleepz, 2012
8. SKIP&DIE—Love Jihad
   (Riots In The Jungle) Crammed Discs, 2012
9. Dio ft. Hadewych Minis—Ze Houdt Van Me
   (Benjamin Braafs Festival) Topnotch, 2012
10. Chef'Special—Biggest Monkey
    (One For The Mrs.) Kaiser, 2011
11. Kroons—Hesitate
    (Single) Kroonsmusic, 2012
12. Netsky—Love Has Gone
    (2) Hospital/N.E.W.S., 2012
13. Oscar And The Wolf—Orange Sky
    (Summer Skin) PIAS Recordings, 2012
14. [illegible]
15. DeWolff—Voodoo Mademoiselle
16. Drums Are For Parades ft. Tim Vanhamel

PRESENTING MIXTAPE 5

[...] Converse Mixtape is in het leven geroepen om [...]mende bands onder de aandacht te brengen [...] onze muziekfans. De Mixtape waarop jong [...] en gevestigde namen elkaar ontmoeten is [...]dels aan de 5e editie toe en dit keer in drie [...]illende versies uitgebracht. Alle 31 artiesten [...] belangeloos een track bijgedragen in de [...]s BEATS, INDIE & ROCK.

[...] Converse winkels kun je deze CD's bemachtigen [...]zijde liefde tussen Converse en muziek. [...] edities zijn gratis te downloaden via [...]converse.nl/mixtape en [...]converse.be/mixtape

[...]ns de CONVERSE NIGHTS vieren we de [...]zijdse liefde tussen Converse en muziek. [...]antal van onze favoriete bands zullen [...]illende gangen door Nederland en België [...]spelen.

[...]aal voor de clubtour is deze limited edition [...]pe samengesteld, waarop je kunt luisteren [...] de zes artiesten die zullen spelen tijdens [...]ERSE NIGHTS. Bereid je voor op een eclec-[...] ontdekkingstocht van de meest uiteen-[...] genres en tracks die de Converse Mixtape [...] 5 te bieden heeft!

TOURDATA

HANDSOME POETS (NL) IMAGINARY FAMILY (BE)

22 NOVEMBER EFFENAAR, EINDHOVEN

BOMBAY SHOW PIG (NL) OSCAR & THE WOLF (BE)

24 NOVEMBER CHARLATAN, GENT

AKS (BE) SKIP&DIE (NL) KROONS (NL)

29 NOVEMBER TRIX, ANTWERPEN

DRIVE LIKE MARIA (NL) DRUMS ARE FOR PARADES (BE)

8 DECEMBER TIVOLI DE HELLING, UTRECHT

OSCAR & THE WOLF

Interview met Max, Filip, Roland en Claudio

Vraag: Wanneer en hoe is jullie muziek ontstaan?
Antwoord: Twee jaar geleden zaten Max en Filip op dezelfde school, het Sint Lucas in Gent. Max stuurde een mailtje naar Filip, en toen hebben we afgesproken om een keer te gaan jammen. Vervolgens zijn we samen ons eerste nummer gaan schrijven.

Vraag: Hoe zouden jullie je muziek omschrijven?
Antwoord: Zuiderse, donkere folkpop en -rock. Het is een apart hokje!

Vraag: Wat vinden jullie ervan dat er vaak altijd om een genre wordt gevraagd, terwijl het vaak onmogelijk lijkt om muziek een definitie te geven?
Antwoord: Je moet muziek in ieder geval een beetje definiëren, zodat mensen weten in welke richting ze kunnen denken. Soms is het jammer als een stempel onjuist of niet effectief is, maar praktisch gezien is het wel handig.

Vraag: Wat is jullie favoriete geluid op aarde? Welk gevoel geeft het jullie?
Antwoord: Een ufo die op aarde landt! Of misschien wel het geluid van een zaag. Instinctief trekt dat me heel erg aan. Het is hoog en fatalistisch, maar toch heel mooi.

Vraag: Wat hopen jullie met muziek te bereiken?
Antwoord: Rijk worden! Nee, serieus, we willen op z'n minst op hetzelfde niveau blijven. Alleen het liefst worden we nog beter.

Vraag: Wat is de ideale plek om naar jullie muziek te luisteren?
Antwoord: Aan het water of in een tram. Of tijdens een bruiloft in Californië, die in een tram plaats-vindt! Dus als je iemand kent die in Californië woont...

Vraag: Wat voor band hebben jullie met Converse?
Antwoord: All Stars waren de eerste schoenen die je als kind echt wilde hebben. Het zijn klassiekers met een hele toffe geschiedenis.

www.oscarandthewolf.com

OSCAR & THE WOLF

BOMBAY SHOW PIG

Interview met Linda en Mathias

Vraag: Wanneer en hoe is jullie band ontstaan?
Antwoord: Wij zijn Bombay Show Pig, een indieduo uit Amsterdam en Den Haag. We hebben ons debuutalbum in mei uitgebracht onder Kytopia. Daar hebben we ook de CD opgenomen. De band is ongeveer drie jaar geleden ontstaan.

Vraag: Hoe zouden jullie je muziek omschrijven?
Antwoord: Als indierock! De plaat heeft invloeden van Arcade Fire en Beck.

Vraag: Wat vinden jullie ervan dat er bijna altijd om een genre wordt gevraagd, terwijl het vaak onmogelijk lijkt om muziek een definitie te geven?
Antwoord: Nou, dat hoort er gewoon een beetje bij. Op een gegeven moment moet je daar steeds vaker antwoord op geven. We snappen wel dat muziek getypeerd moet worden.

Vraag: Wat is de ideale plek om naar jullie muziek te luisteren?
Antwoord: Live, tijdens van onze shows. Misschien klinkt onze volgende clubtour? Het album is heel wel geworden, maar in concert benaderen we muziek op een hele andere manier. Ik vind het altijd leuk om een band te zien die de nummers live op een andere manier vertolkt en op die manier een nieuwe dimensie vindt.

Vraag: Wat hopen jullie met je muziek te bereiken?
Antwoord: We willen graag in zoveel mogelijk landen een basis hebben, zodat we niet alleen in Nederland, maar ook in de rest van Europa en Amerika kunnen spelen. Zo kom je tenminste op vette plekken! We zijn net terug van een tour door Zuid-Afrika, en we hebben al een tour door de Balkan gemaakt. Ook hebben we in Duitsland gespeeld en gaan we nog naar Frankrijk. Tijdens Converse Nights spelen we in Nederland én België!

BOMBAY SHOW PIG

Vraag: Wat voor band hebben jullie met Converse?
Antwoord: We dragen al twee jaar lang All Stars. Ze zitten fijn en passen overal bij. Toen we nog maar net begonnen met spelen, had Converse ons al gespot. Heel tof.

Vraag: Wat is jullie grootste schoenenmiskoop ooit?
Antwoord: Linda: Plateauzolen in de jaren 90? Dat was geen succes! En slippers die na een dag dragen al kapot gaan.
Mathias: Oh, gympen uit China! Na twee keer dragen pas je met twee voeten in een schoen.

www.bombayshowpig.com

SKIP&DIE

Interview met Cata.Pirata

Vraag: Wanneer en hoe is jullie band ontstaan?
Antwoord: SKIP&DIE is een paar jaar geleden ontstaan als samenwerking tussen Jori Collignon, onze producer, en mij. We besloten om naar Zuid-Afrika te gaan om daar muziek op te nemen. Toen we terugkwamen beseften we dat het veel leuker zou zijn als we een grotere groep zouden worden, met meer bandleden. Stukje bij beetje hebben we elkaar ontmoet, en sinds ongeveer een half jaar zijn we met z'n vijven.

Vraag: Hoe zou je jullie muziek omschrijven?
Antwoord: Als een tropisch avontuur!

Vraag: Wat vind je ervan dat er bijna altijd om een genre wordt gevraagd, terwijl het vaak onmogelijk lijkt om muziek een definitie te geven?
Antwoord: Mensen houden er nou eenmaal van om dingen in hokjes te plaatsen. Ik vind niet dat mijn muziek in een specifiek genre geplaatst hoeft te worden, maar ik zou het wel als tropical bass omschrijven. Ook al kennen veel mensen dat genre niet, kan ik het zo toch in een soort context zien.

Vraag: Wat is je favoriete geluid op aarde? Welk gevoel geeft het je?
Antwoord: Het geluid van de golven. Wat ik ook heel leuk vind is het geluid dat krekels 's nachts maken. Dat is een heel rustgevend geluid.

Vraag: Wat hoop je met jullie muziek te bereiken?
Antwoord: Ik wil mezelf in ieder geval op een creatieve manier beter leren kennen. En als band willen we natuurlijk steeds meer en beter gaan spelen. Deze muziek is waar ik van houd en ik gebruik het als uitlaatklep. Ik zou niet weten wat ik anders moest doen, dus we gaan heel duurzaam zo door!

Vraag: Wat is de ideale plek om naar jullie muziek te luisteren?
Antwoord: Live is misschien wel het beste. Daar vind je veel positieve energie. Je kan bewegen en het is echt feest. Ons album is wel een luister-plaat, dus als je op roadtrip gaat, zou je er in de auto naar kunnen luisteren als voorbereiding op je avontuur.

Vraag: Wat voor band hebben jullie met Converse?
Antwoord: Converse heeft altijd wel iets met muziek en toffe artiesten. Waar ik echt gek op ben zijn de platform All Stars, die binnenkort uitkomen.

www.skipndie.com

SKIP&DIE

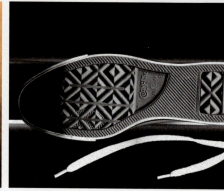

MAGINARY FAMILY

Interview met Joanna

Wie is de vrouw achter Imaginary Family?
Antwoord: Mijn naam is Joanna. Ik ben 26 jaar en in Gent. Drie jaar geleden begon ik met gitaarspelen. De band om mij heen bestaat uit twee mensen, die allebei heel veel instrumenten bespelen. Eigenlijk bestaat de band pas een paar weken, in mijn eentje gebruikte ik al een tijdje deze naam.

Hoe zou je jullie muziek omschrijven?
Antwoord: Ik zou het indiefolk of new folk noemen.

Wat vind je ervan dat er bijna altijd om een genre wordt gevraagd, terwijl het vaak onmogelijk lijkt om muziek een definitie te geven?
Antwoord: Ik vind het niet erg, ook al is het wel lastig. Mensen zijn altijd naar vragen. Ik ben nu eenmaal zo bezig met genres. Als ik zeg dat ik een singer-songwriter ben, zou het zomaar kunnen dat ik verdrietige nummers maak over mislukte liefdes. Dat is niet zo. Ik ben eerder een sound artist.

Vraag: Wat hoop je met jullie muziek te bereiken?
Antwoord: Ik probeer vooral goede muziek te maken, die ik zelf heel leuk vind. Hopelijk vinden anderen dat ook!

Vraag: Wat is je favoriete geluid op aarde? Welk gevoel geeft het je?
Antwoord: Daar moet ik even over nadenken. Ik houd van het geluid dat een oude typemachine maakt. Ik heb zelf nooit een typemachine gehad, maar het heeft iets nostalgisch.

Vraag: Wat is de ideale plek om naar jullie muziek te luisteren?
Antwoord: Ik luister zelf graag naar muziek in de trein, dus een doodstille nachttrein zou een goede plek zijn.

Vraag: Wat is je grootste schoenenmiskoop ooit?
Antwoord: Toen ik elf jaar oud was, heb ik gouden schoenen gekocht. Ik was er zelf heel blij mee, maar misschien vonden de mensen om mij heen het wel een miskoop.

www.imaginaryfamily.com

KROONS

Interview met Lula Ross

Vraag: Kan je wat vertellen over Kroons?
Antwoord: Kroons is zo'n zee jaar geleden ontstaan. Als duo (zangeres Lula Ross en MC Unannounced Guest) werken we samen met verschillende producers en muzikanten.

Vraag: Hoe zouden jullie je muziek omschrijven?
Antwoord: Dat is een moeilijke vraag! Er zit van alles in onze muziek: hiphop, pop met een rauw randje en wat elementen van triphop. Eigenlijk is het heel breed.

Vraag: Wat vind je ervan dat er bijna altijd om een genre wordt gevraagd, terwijl het vaak onmogelijk lijkt om muziek een definitie te geven?
Antwoord: Ik vind het omschrijven van muziek altijd heel moeilijk; muziek moet je horen. Als je er woorden aan hangt, zegt dat vaak weinig. Kroons staat juist voor het loslaten van grenzen,

en over grenzen heengaan. Onze liveshow is behalve voor mijzelf ook voor het publiek heel uitdagend. Het leven wordt vaak opgedeeld in hokjes, maar wij willen dat juist loslaten. Muziek kan je niet begrenzen door het een naam te geven.

Vraag: Wat is de ideale plek om naar jullie muziek te luisteren?
Antwoord: Onze liveshows! Daarin krijg je helemaal mee wat we willen zeggen. Dat gevoel krijg je pas echt als je bij een concert bent.

Vraag: Wat hoop je met jullie muziek te bereiken?
Antwoord: We hebben verschillende doelen. Wat we willen meegeven als muzikanten is een verhaal. En waar we over vertellen is een complete vrijheid, zoals het loslaten van patronen en het kind in jezelf de ruimte gunnen.

Vraag: Wat is je grootste schoenenmiskoop ooit?
Antwoord: Ooi! Ik heb ooit tweedehands pumps gekocht. Ze waren heel leuk, maar ik kon er absoluut niet op lopen. Ze maakten me ook heel lomp, terwijl pumps juist elegant horen te zijn.

Vraag: Wat is je favoriete geluid op aarde?
Antwoord: Ik word heel blij van het geluid van hagelslag die uit het tuitje van het pak op mijn brood valt. Daar ben ik aan verslaafd. En het geluid van de douche – ook heel fijn!

www.kroons.nl

DRIVE LIKE MARIA

Interview met Nitzan

Kan je wat over jullie band vertellen en hoe is Drive Like Maria ontstaan?
Antwoord: Drive Like Maria is ontstaan als reden een groep vrienden om een feestje in rock-'n-roll te bouwen. Bjorn en ik leerden elkaar kennen in studio in Hilversum. Kort daarna ik naar Hasselt om zijn soloplaat op te nemen. We hoorden over een wedstrijd die rond de Melkweg, begonnen een band en liep het met wat vrienden naar Amsterdam. Tot onze grote verbazing wonnen we en hoorden een paar dagen later in Londen de wereldwijde finale zou plaatsvinden, en we mee zouden dingen naar de hoofdprijs van 100.000 dollar! We werden vierde en wonnen dus niet het bedrag, maar wel optreden in Mexico City. Ineens hadden we een band.

Hoe zou je jullie muziek omschrijven?
Antwoord: Moeilijk! Ik zeg meestal rock, alternatieve rock of stonerpop. Kies maar.

Vraag: Vind je het lastig dat er bijna altijd om een genre wordt gevraagd, terwijl het vaak onmogelijk lijkt om muziek een definitie te geven?
Antwoord: Ik snap wel dat het voor mensen handig is om te weten in welk vakje ze het kunnen thuisbrengen. Als we worden vergeleken met andere bands zijn dat meestal allemaal hele goede bands, dus dan voel ik me alleen maar vereerd.

Vraag: Wat is de ideale plek om naar jullie muziek te luisteren?
Antwoord: In de auto.

Vraag: Wat hopen jullie met je muziek te bereiken?
Antwoord: We willen natuurlijk veel spelen en veel mensen bereiken, maar we maken de muziek niet met een doel. We maken de muziek omdat mooie muziek maken voor ons het doel op zich is.

Vraag: Wat voor band heb je met Converse?
Antwoord: We hebben al sinds de release van ons eerste album een goede band met Converse. Ik droog sowieso al vaak All Stars.

Vraag: Wat is je grootste schoenenmiskoop ooit?
Antwoord: Die heb ik al vertrongen! Ik weet niet eens meer hoe ze eruit zagen, maar heb ze weggegeven en er niet meer aan gedacht.

Vraag: Wat is je favoriete geluid op aarde? Welk gevoel geeft het je?
Antwoord: Donder... Een hele fijne dreun ik vind storm echt heerlijk.

www.drivelike...

JOOST VANDEBRUG

Joost Vandebrug laat zich niet afschrikken door de werkelijkheid. Rauwe portretten en gruizige rock-'n-roll kenmerken zijn oeuvre. De fotograaf en filmregisseur, die vroeger graag rockster wilde worden, groeide op in een klein dorpje in Friesland. Doordat de bandjes van zijn vrienden vaak foto's nodig hadden, was hij al op jonge leeftijd bezig met het ontwikkelen van zijn talent. Na de middelbare school studeerde Vandebrug aan de Gerrit Rietveld Academie in Amsterdam, waar hij ook stage liep bij Erwin Olaf. Muziek speelt nog steeds een belangrijke rol in het werk van de fotograaf; hij laat zich graag inspireren door de punkbands. In de afgelopen jaren schoot Vandebrug campagnes voor onder andere Dries Van Noten, Iris van Herpen en Rick Owens. Ook werkte hij voor magazines als Vogue Italia, V Man, Glamcult en Dazed & Confused.

www.joostvandebrug.com

CONVERSE THNX

Alle bands, labels en management die de Mixtape mogelijk maken. Unleash the creative spirit.

CONVERSE

www.converse.nl/mixtape
www.converse.be/mixtape

GLAMCULT INDEPENDENT STYLE PAPER
DESIGN: GLAMCULT STUDIO

Since the release of the magazine in 2003, Glamcult has developed itself from an edgy underground tabloid to one of the leading independent magazines in the Netherlands when it comes to fashion, music, film, art and today's youth culture. Glamcult offers its readers articles on and interviews with the hottest fashion designers, artists, musicians, actors and photographers on a monthly basis, looking way beyond mainstream culture.

It is not Glamcult's aim to tell their readers what to wear, what music to listen to or which parties to attend. Their readers know very well what they want and what is happening around them. They are the innovators and create their own world. Glamcult just gives them a broad impression of what is going on in the frontlines of fashion, art, music and film. They select, create and wonder around in today's avant-garde cultures and present it with strong visual language, attractive content and an expressive imagery.

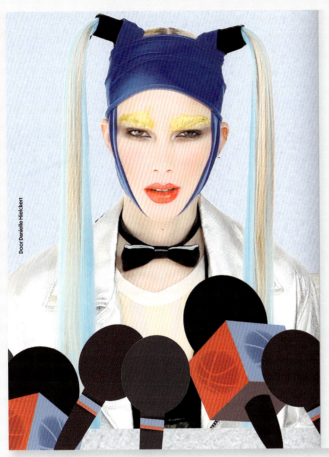

Door Danielle Hielckert

Reed + Rader

"Cats are the greatest people in the world. They are furry little bosses. They are the masterminds behind our work", aldus Pamela Reed en Matthew Rader. De twee vormen samen het kunstenaarsduo Reed + Rader uit New York, succesvol geworden dankzij hun liefde voor elkaar en een gedeelde passie voor computerspelletjes, technologie... en katten dus. Het koppel verandert het modebeeld graag door *high fashion* looks te gebruiken in hun eigen gecreëerde sprookjeswerelden, waarin Super Mario het opneemt tegen dinosaurussen en geisha's achterna gezeten worden door pacman-achtige wezens.

Still-pictures uit de serie look form, 2012.

35   Gc Interview

Tom Van Der Borght

2013 nam een snelle start voor de Gentse ontwerper Tom Van Der Borght. Hij stampte zijn eigen label uit de grond en won meteen ook de Premium Young Designers Award met zijn eerste collectie tijdens Berlin Fashion Week. Dit kwam niet als een hele grote verrassing, want zijn eclectische en kleurrijke stijl liet ook al het nakijken tijdens zijn studie aan de Stedelijke Academie voor Schone Kunsten in Sint-Niklaas.

Door Ianthe De Boeck
Fotografie: Tini Cleemput

"Het is look ook ik meteen kan inspireren. Soms gebeurt dat heel dichtbij mij. Mijn richten van acht jaar inwoxite dit inzien zelf, geïnspireerd op mijn collectie The Church of Chaos. De appel valt niet ver van de boom"

In dit ontwerp heeft Tom het bootstype van zijn ziekte in een bevoqwerglijke sportschoen verwerkt.

"Ik werk eerst alleen en pas it in kleine scrapbook. De ideeën die hierin tot stand komt vertel het vervoorgaanst voor de uiteindelijke collectie."

Door voorwerpen los te raken uit hun context en samen te brengen tot een nieuw geheel komt Tom tot verrassende beelden. "Dit zijn kleine hebbedingen die ik kreeg van vrienden, en doel uitmaken van mijn immer veranderende interieur"

Chica, Toms hond die het elegantgezice vormde voor de spring-summer 2015 collectie The Church of Chaos

Met een couplexe en patroonuitier per zijn mode, kwam Tom Van Der Borght al van jongs af aan in contact met de creatieve zelf. Hij volgde de sprong naar de modewereld achter pas na jaren aan de ervaring te hebben ingenomen in de sociale sector. In het laatste jaar daarvan, toen hij zich nare te voor achtergestelde jongeren, kwam Tom erachter dat hij aan de artistieke uiter media Chanal Marie Toorti fjcit Walerks griechad door dit tebouw dorf de tijd te kiezen voor zijn grote passie mode. "Ontwerpen is voor mij zelf ook een soort sociaal project ik uit er de wereld beter door Van ziekim".

Tna nas de griezgan-van gevel facie schoonheidsidealen dit elkedad weerstand tegen algemeen aanvaarde

conventies. Zijn allitatieexcollectie The Church of Chaos is een manifest tegen het modebeeld dat vandaag de dag heivig wordt gehomoplaneerd. Hij ging hierroot op onderzoek naar de historie van seksten en vond een oversserkomst na het vica vith verbaugen koorde honi per net de mode. Het haarestatil moge bereikt bag mensen schoonheidsidelaan. op, het raadt een wete haar leden een en ersauilso dicteert. "Ik vind het proces voor bezongrijker dan het resultaat. Ik ken melt zelf eerst bezig met onderzoek dan met design, vertelt de omwerper.

Tom put zoo veel biospecile uit zijn eigen keren. "Het kost me grieppig om een serisbt ISAS Plan nuitsui uit in kenden. Op die manner veranderten ik

mijn schatge, sinpele hand tot iets kunstaardige," in de omwerper uit deze Gentse berweergen gaan hand werk, borduren en brodeuneris hand in hand met moderne, industriële prin en onderbreken. Voor elk look gaat hij op zoek naar voornemewikringen die Liju zee e utbanee en uitentranen. "Ik kan het vergelijken met muziek, te heeft mensen die leven het origineel hasm, maar ik kan heel genieed van remixen. Het geheel krijgt daardoor meerdere lagen en stijlen, die het look zou hebben als het gemaakt zor die door een enkel persoon", aldus Tom.

tomvandenborght.com

26   Gc Platform

Interviews

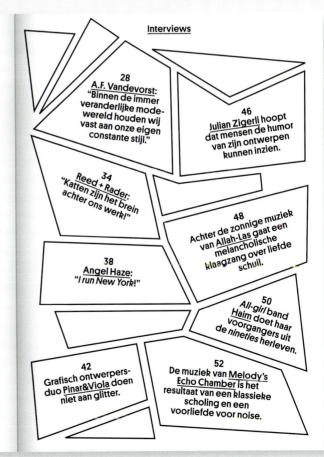

Ze draaien alweer een hele poos mee in de modewereld. An Vandevorst en Filip Arickx ontmoetten elkaar op hun eerste schooldag aan de Koninklijke Academie voor Schone Kunsten in Antwerpen in 1987. Intussen is hun logo wereldberoemd en prijkt hun werk zowel in musea als in toonaangevende boetieks. "Het fijne aan mode is dat het constant in beweging is. Als iets bijzonders ons pad kruist, dan gaan we ervoor."

28

29   Gc Interview

De eerste en de laatste collectie, die zijn altijd het mooist, vinden An en Filip. Hun eerste collectie presenteerden ze in 1998 in Parijs en ze sleepten er onmiddellijk de Venus de la Mode Award mee in de wacht. Sindsdien keerde de combinatie van zachte, delicate lingerie-elementen met harde leren harnassen en militaire vilten jassen herhaaldelijk in hun werk terug. Ook hun fascinatie voor uniformen, Rusland en het werk van de kunstenaar Joseph Beuys is vanaf het begin een grote inspiratiebron geweest. Er zijn maar weinig labels die al in zo'n vroeg stadium een eigen signatuur neerzetten. De meest recente collectie van A.F. Vandevorst voor spring/summer 2013 gaat over de overgang van winter naar zomer. Dat zie je terug in het kleurgebruik—van licht naar donker in monochroom, wat typisch is voor de ontwerpen van het duo— en in het silhouet dat evolueert van zwaar naar licht. Het is een vervolg op de najaarscollectie, waarbij de modellen zich als een soort spionnen in hun outfits verschoten. "Ditmaal wilden we wat frisse en positieve benadrukken", leggen An en Filip uit. "Ze is nog steeds

mysterieus en draagt nog altijd een hoed, maar is duidelijk extraverter." Werden de gezichten van de modellen vorig seizoen nog afgeschermd door zware vilten fedora's, dit keer zorgden transparante gazhoeden juist voor een gevoel van lichtheid. De luxe schakel den hiervoor opnieuw de hulp in van Stephen Jones. Een minimalistisch ontwerp voor zijn doen: de bekendste Britse hoedenmaker staat bekend als 'mad hatter'. "Geweldig", zei hij toen An en Filip het hem voorstelden. "Het idee is eigenlijk zo simpel, dat ik daar niet eerder op ben gekomen." Tijdens het defilé waren de handen en gezichten van de modellen of zelfs hun volledige bovenlijf verguld. "Het goud staat voor optimisme, feestelijkheid gaat de collectie ook over dressing up. In welke periode was dat vooral belangrijk, vroegen we ons af. Dan kom je al snel uit bij de Gouden Eeuw. Het viel ons op dat het accent in die periode heel erg op de taille lag. Ook het gebruik van handschoenen refereert aan die stijlperiode." De afgelopen seizoenen toonde A.F. Vandevorst een minder clean beeld

dan we van ze gewend waren en de baroke invloeden nemen toe. Dat ze een andere koers zijn de ontwerpers zich bewust. "Ons werk oogt minder leidelijk", aldus Filip. Tegelijkertijd benadrukken ze dat er geen plan achter zit. "We laten ons gewoon ont- wikkelen. Mode geeft ons een groot huis. Daarvan hangt soms nadelig zijn, maar onze creativiteit heeft nu eenmaal kunnen autonome kleur." Misschien is dat ook een reden dat A.F. Vandevorst het dit jaar in de museumwereld: zijn dit jaar te zien in het Red—Fashion Victim bekend in Hasselt, papieren juwelen af van het ter ziele gegane Paris(ian Fashion en het Fashion besteedt ook aandacht aan samenwerkingen met bekende modeontwerpers en makers. An: "Een mode- een andere podium dat we minder pochtig. Bezoekers ervaren dat kleding stilleging en te kijken als ze zelf willen. Wij...

30

Boven: H&M, Haar Monique van Heist. Onder: Paul Smith. Haar Hans Intraats, schoenen Nelly.

the good guys.

Styling: Jordy Huinder—Eric Elenbaas Agency
Haar en make-up: Dennis Michael—Angelique Hoorn Management voor
Ella Faas Cosmetics en Kevin Murphy
Model: Leenden
Assistenten fotografie: Humphrey Kibauw en Kim Nicolai
Alle kleding: Julian Zigerli spring/summer 2013

Door Leenden Sonnevelt
Fotografie: Marco van Rijt—Eric Elenbaas Agency

een eralage, briefpapier—het Rode
Kruis heeft een paar keer op de stoep
gestaan met hun vriendelijke verzoek
hun logo niet meer te gebruiken. Sindsdien is het kruis een subtiele belijning in
de vorm van een rood stiksel op stof.
A.F. Vandevorst noem enige tijd geleden
een nieuwe grafisch ontwerper in de
arm. Hij bouwt voor op de bestaande
beeldelementen van Marc Meulemans,
die jarenlang de huisontwerper van het
modeduo was. Filip: "Hij had een man
met enorm veel ervaring. Hij had een
brede achtergrond en was behalve met
mode en grafische vormgeving ook heel
bekend met muziek en shows. Nu werken
we met veel jonger iemand. Dat
is niet zuiver beter of slechter, maar anders. Het zorgt voor een frisse wind,
hoeveel de huisstijl redelijk consequent
is. Merchandising is altijd zuur eno-
tioneel, want verpakkingen zijn simpelweg bedoeld om er mooi uit te zien."

Het moeie voor de ontwerper als
een gelukzomoment wanneer iets eruit
ziet zoals hij het in zijn hoofd had. Dat
gebeurt gelukkig dikwijls. "Soms wordt
je heel erg bij van een specifiek item,

Julian Zigerli

kennismaking met Julian Zigerli kan simpelweg niet
aan. "I've *always* been the guy with the weird stuff", begint
Zwitserse modeontwerper. "Humor vind ik heel belang-
o dat mensen in lachen uitbarsten als ze mijn moodboards
en." Zo optimistisch als Zigerli zelf is ook zijn werk. De
annencollecties worden gekenmerkt door grafische prints
ortieve, hypermoderne uitstraling. "Misschien wel té
idus de ontwerper. "Mensen houden ervan of ze vinden
welijk. Een middenweg bestaat niet."

technicolor
iel van zijn
atie echter
"Op een
iip. "Ik zag
an. En ook al
der de vorm-
v eigenlijk is."
fRof werd de
ectie. "Vergis
atisch. Ik heb
de elementen
ingen. Insane!"
il die grafisch
voor mode
gt totaal ze
"Daarom
eenlig voor
ubben." "Tegen-
erper weer in

zijn thuisstad Zürich. Toch toont hij zijn
collectie nog steeds in de Duitse hoofd-
stad. "Het is mijn tweede thuis, maar de
stad heeft een overdosis aan modeontwerpers. In Zwitserland is de scene
heel klein, er waarom zou je daar geen
gebruik van maken om je eigen label
op te bouwen?"

Zigerli toont zijn creaties het
liefst op zoveel mogelijk plekken. Of hij
een favoriete stad heeft? "Absoluut niet!"
reageert hij verbaasd. "Als er echt
maar één stad geschikt zou zijn voor
mijn ontwerpen, zou ik vandaag nog
kunnen stoppen met werken. Het leuke
is wel dat iedere plek een zichtbare
voorkeur heeft. Zo zijn ze in Japan gek
op de prints, terwijl in Zwitserland de
rustige stukken juist worden gewaar-
deerd." Zijn najaar/winter 2012 collectie
toonde Zigerli in Londen als onderdeel
van Vauxhall Fashion Scout. Een mooie
en kansrijke stad, althans de ontwerper.
"Londen is vooral gericht op ontwerpers
die daar wonen, waardoor het voor
'buitenstaanders' moeilijk is om voet aan
de grond te krijgen. Dit jaar ben ik naar
New York gegaan voor mijn Amerikaan-
se showroomdebuut." Hij zijt het even
en gaat dan verder. "Er is nog een reden
dat ik naar New York wilde. Het heeft
iets te maken met mijn nieuwe film, naar

meer kan ik daar nu niet over loslaten!"

Naast de aerodynamische invloe-
den van zijn werk, toont Zigerli's collectie ook een duidelijk versatzschap met
sport. De ontwerper grinnikt. "Dat klopt
van humor. Natuurlijk heeft iedereen een
duistere kant, maar waarom zij mensen
daar zo gefascineerd door? Why nor
make your wardrobe a happy place?"

De zorgeloze sfeer in Zigerli's
ontwerpen wordt niet alleen beïnvloed
door Japanse anime. De mannencollec-
ties van Prada en Balenciaga houden
de ontwerper ieder seizoen weer bezig.
"Balenciaga is super modern, daar houd
ik van, maar natuurlijk roept het bij veel
mensen ook weerstand op." Het heden-
daagse kent ieng in Zigerli's eigen
prints, die anderen ontwerpen in samenwerking met een Berlijnse kunstenaar.
"Via Skype heb ik het idee achter de
collectie aan hem uitgelegd. Inmiddels
heb ik het resultaat al zo vaak gezien
dat ik liever aan mijn nieuwe collectie
denk", lacht Zigerli. "Misschien vind je
de prints wel te modern. Mensen houden
ervan of ze vinden het afschuwelijk, een
middenweg bestaat niet. Ergens begrijp
ik dat wel. Maar als ik over een jaar te-
rugkijk, weet ik zeker dat ik denk: 'Wow,
that's pretty amazing!'"

www.julianzigerli.com

stelt hij bevligen. "Ken je de regisseur
Hayao Miyazaki? In zijn films komt nooit
een antagonist voor, dat vind ik geweldig. Nij soort mode is blij, het getuigt

---

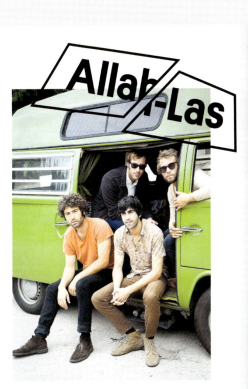

Door Fay Breeman
Fotografie: Jennie Warren

De leden van Allah-Las leerden elkaar
kennen toen ze werkten bij Amoeba, een
platenzaak met een reputatie die stand-
plaats Los Angeles ver oversteigt. Je hoeft
niet lang naar hun zelfgetitelde debuut-
plaat te luisteren om te vermoeden dat
Miles Michaud (leadvocalen en gitaar),
Pedrum Siadatian (leadgitaar en vocalen), Spencer Dunham (bas en vocalen)
en Matthew Correia (drum en vocalen)
inspiratie opdeden tussen Amoeba's
rekken vol tweedehands vinyl. De kennis-
die de somenzang, galmende gitaren
en rijkelijk rommelende tamboerijn van
de nummers af L.T.- then kent denken aan
de zonnige melodieën van hun muzikale
collega's uit de jaren 60. Dan hebben
we het vooral over de surfpop van
The Beach Boys en de psychedelica van
The Byrds—het voor niets afkomstig uit
dezelfde stad—en over een klein vleugje
bossa nova. Dat de apparatuur waar-
mee de mannen in samenwerking met
nu-revivalist Nick Waterhouse hun album
opnamen, net zo oud is als het muzikale
tijdperk waar hun sound naar verwijst,
draagt des te meer bij aan dit gevoel.
Tel daarbij op de videoclips van de
band er allemaal uitzien alsof ze in een
vervlogen tijd op analoge film zijn opgenomen, dan is het niet zo verwonder-
lijk dat alle artikelen over Allah-Las vol
staan met woorden als 'sixties', 'vintage'
en 'retro'.

Verrassend genoeg is zelfs de
keuze voor het opnemen op tape, die zo
bepalend is voor de kleur en het gevoel
van het eerste Allah-Las-album, op een
of meer toevallige wijze tot stand gekomen. De band begon ooit met het digitaal opnemen van hun nummers, maar
het resultaat daarvan kon hen niet be-
koren. Matthew: "Muziek wordt digitaal
opgenomen, zodat het beluisterd kan
worden op cd. Maar wij wilden ons album opnemen om beluisterd te worden
op vinyl." De plaat werd dus niet digitaal
vastgelegd en is vanaf doorgrocht
naar een betere registratietechniek.
Vriend Nick Waterhouse
stelde voor om in zijn studio The Distillery,
ten zuiden van L.A. een aan beginnen
te proberen. Het was daar tussen de
jukeboxen en obscure apparaten van
welleer dat eindelijk het juiste geluid
werd gevonden. Matthew: "Open is een
ingeschikkelde manier om een stuk ge-
te nemen, maar voor ons was dat de
betere. Het brengt bepaalde elementen
in de muziek naar boven die anders niet
ze komen."

Allah-Las

Als een band niet op zoek is naar een vast
gekunstelde samenhang tussen muziek, v
eigenlijk probeert te vermijden, kan er too
pakket van geluid, beeld en gevoel tot sta
geval bij de 4-koppige formatie Allah-Las
het analoge tijdperk—en dan voornamelijk e
lijkt te komen. Dat de band in kwestie daar n
blij mee is, bleek toen Glamcult de manne

decennium geschreven kunnen. We
worden heel vaak weggezet als ze
jaren-60 band, terwijl dat maar een frac
tie is van wat we zijn. Ik vind dat gewoon
luie journalistiek." Hoewel Spencer meer
een uitgesproken en pegt dat die kritiek
natuurlijk wel voor de 60ertjesgeest
bedoeld is, is duidelijk dat de mannen
het niet helemaal eens zijn met de
manier waarop er in de pers worden be-
schreven. Kennelijk is het plaatje van een
vintage band, met al die uitingen van
Allah-Las zo bewust en vol overtuiging
lijkt neergezet, eigenlijk een openstac-
peling van toevallige uitjes tot stand gekomen, die 60er op L.A. hun veroroll
niet bedoeld waren om zich een retro
imago aan te meten.

De cover van Als-s geserveerd
en is prachtige en... di
Daar prijkt een—he
analoog en wordige
de middaels bepassd
graaf David Hamilto
exotische sfeer die g
gene schep legt; je
legt, werd onlangs o
gebruikt voor de cove
een album van Van de
Taken by Trees, dat to
kertijd met das met s
In waarvoor de van de
Van The Concretes son
toevallig—het nou
van The Beach Br
van Other Worlds een
het werk van Hamilto
Las gekozen om het
te laten. "We wilden
mogelijk eikenrvisieg
zijn bio dan ook nie
Photoshop of iets de
Matthew: Hoewel he
de cover vanuit een
gave van de themab
moest zijn, omraamd
zee en het strand pa
Want metaaa
dat de onderwerpen a
het voornaamste on
de mannen bezig g

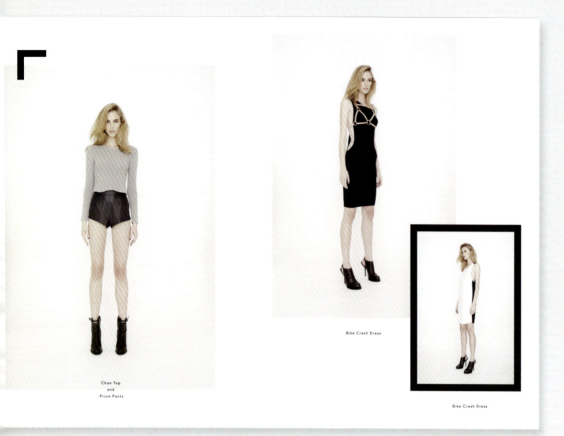

Chan Top
and
Prism Pants

Bike Crash Dress

Lafayette Knit

Bike Crash Dress

Stardust Leather Dress

Nana Shirt
and
Stardust Leather Skirt

Designed for Australian fashion label Friend of Mine, the lookbook makes use of modern shapes to draw focus to the angular and geometric themes of the collection "Ladies Do Not Lean Against Lamp Posts".

Skeleton Dress & Playboy Harness

Stardust Leather Dress

FRIEND
OF MINE

SEASON ONE

Chan Top
and
Prism Pants

Nana Shirt
and
Ziggy Skirt

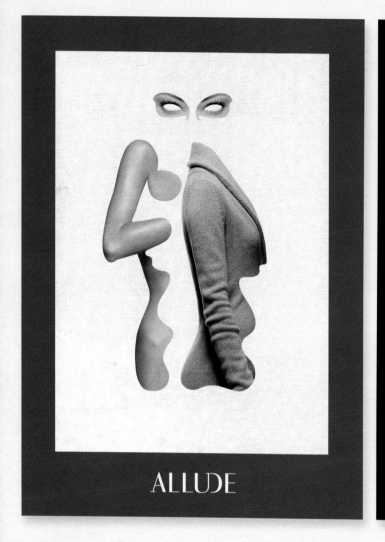

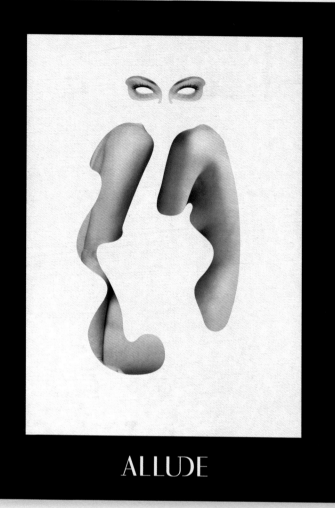

Fall/Winter visual campaign for German cashmere brand Allude.

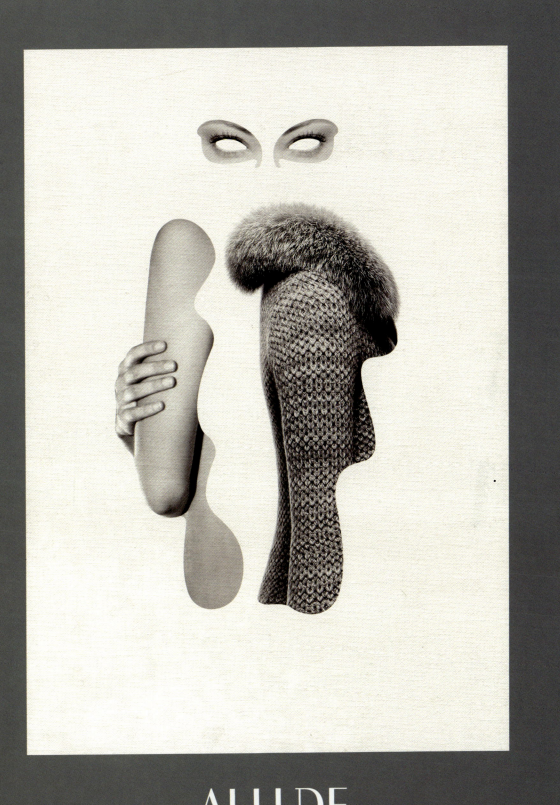

ALLUDE

HOUSE OF LIZA
GRAPHIC DESIGN: KISSMIKLOS
INTERIOR DESIGN: TORSTEN NEELAND
PHOTOGRAPHY: JONHATON GRIGGS

A BOUTIQUE HOUSIN
PIECES OF FASHION

9 PEARSON STREET
LONDON E2 8JD

11am - 6pm Monday

FASHION ARCHIV
André Courrèges
Christian Lacroix
Claude Montana
Comme des Garç
Gianni Versace
Issey Miyake
Jesn-Charles de
Jean Paul Gaultie
Kansai Yamamo
Moschino
Stephen Sprous
Thierry Mugler
Walter Van Bei
&+

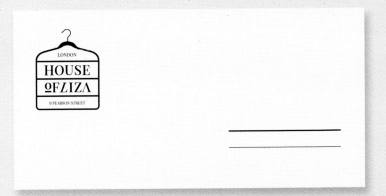

Established in 2010, House of Liza is a boutique that sells handpicked expertly curated pieces of vintage clothing from designers who were experimental and pioneering in previous decades. Recently it introduced a brand new identity design by kissmiklos.

kissmiklos wanted to create a strong concept that would reflect the ethos of House of Liza. His starting point based on the unusual yet simple and effective display system and the vast, white shop with clean lines and a contemporary feel, clothes displayed on a series of lined coat hangers hanging from the ceiling. He knows that the new visual identity has to be as elegant, fashionable and as strong as the new venue. One of the basic elements of the interior design is the coat hanger reflecting fashion and vintage and the shape of the logo recalls the name plates of old shops as it also shows the place of operation.

A BOUTIQUE HOUSING
PIECES OF FASHION HISTORY

9 PEARSON STREET
LONDON E2 8JD

11am – 6pm Monday to Saturday

FASHION ARCHIVE
André Courrèges
Christian Lacroix
Claude Montana
Comme des Garçons
Gianni Versace
Issey Miyake
Jesn-Charles de Castelbajac
Jean Paul Gaultier
Kansai Yamamoto
Moschino

www.houseofliza.co.uk / www.facebook.com/housel

BRANDING HOUSE OF LIZA

Inspired by the joys of wanderlust, Triologie – a fashion label founded by three friends – is conceived for the modern female who lives to discover and enrich her life with fresh experiences.

The three irregular circles in the logo are designed to evoke the feelings of wanderlust: An Appreciation of the next destination; Exploration of its culture, arts, sights and sounds, and finally; a sense of Relaxation from rejuvenation.

To further reflect the brand's free spirit, the circles are placed randomly as if floating away from the wordmark.

Atelier LaDurance
LES BAUX DE PROVENCE

HANDMADE TOPGRAIN LEATHER BELT

INCHES	30/32	32/34	34/36
CM	85	90	95

CEINTURE DE CUIR DE QUALITE FAITE A LA MAIN

There is a remarkable red thread of inventive, lo-tec and inexpensive packaging designs that ties the brand identity of Atelier LaDurance together. Like 'the repairkit' which is attached to all denim products and is assembled with only 'off-the-shelf' metal components. Containing a thimble, two buttons, a piece of pocket lining and a piece of denim. A big image of this brand identifier was used on the silver colored box of the Limited Edition series for the famous Parisian concept store Colette. Other samples are the leather belt packaging: a simple sheet of machine coated white board, folded around the belt and attached with two brass split pens. Or the small cardboard hangtags that indicate the fabric cloth's weight of the Japanese denim product. As the identity program extended across different disciplines, the determination of the brands' overall appearance also included point of sale designs. Like the wooden washboard: a site specific medium and illustrates the brand's product expertise in a narrative way.

Atelier LaDurance
LES BAUX DE PROVENCE

日本のデニム
JAPANESE DENIM

ANETT HAJDU
DESIGN: KISSMIKLOS

A young fashion designer girl's identity design and the 2011-12 Autumn-Winter Accessoires Collection's packaging design.

Anett Hajdu's Accessoires Collection Concept: In the chaos caused by contemporary and eclectic fashion trends, it is a pleasant feeling to turn toward to the style of puritanism what inspired by the nature and people costumes who are living with the nature. People and their everyday objects, animals and the atmosphere around the Arctic Circle provided a starting point for this design collection. Every single bag contains a unique individuality in hidden leather-jewels that helps us to perform as a part of the pure nature. These bags reveals the hidden animal from us.

All the bags are made of cow leather.

The packaging concept fits for the main design theory. The casing reminds us for the meat industrial wrappings, the hunter accessories as well as a little Scandinavian sense.

Gift Certificate Nº

Date of issue

Voucher is redeemable at The Eye Place only. Redemption must be made in full. Multiple vouchers can be combined.
Voucher is valid for two years from date of issue. Only original vouchers accompanied by an official serial number
and signature will be accepted. The Eye Place reserves the right to reject any voucher deemed invalid.

EYE
PLACE

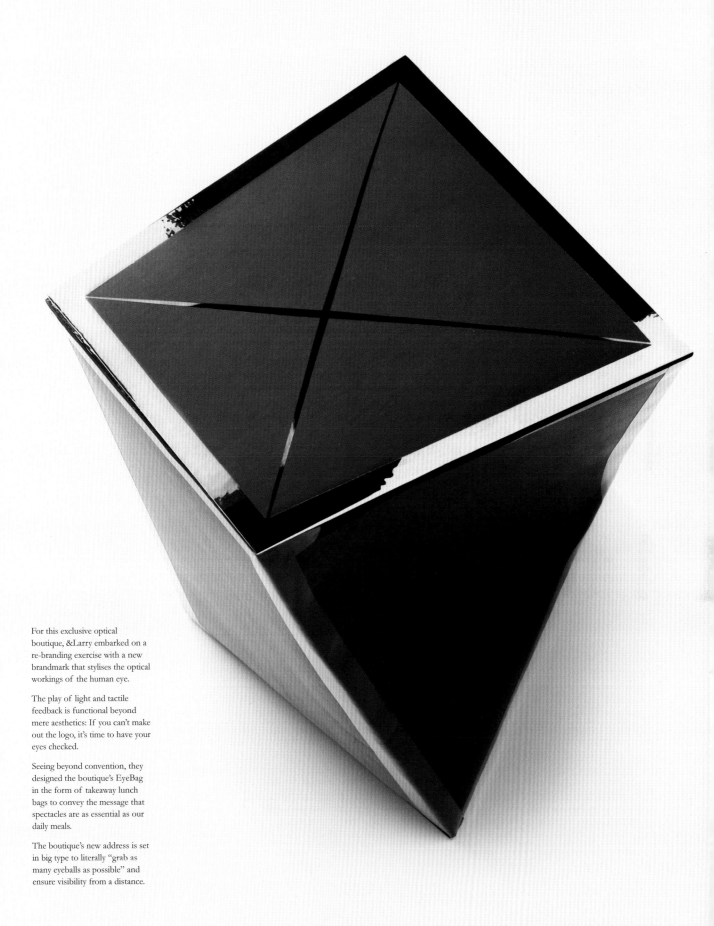

For this exclusive optical boutique, &Larry embarked on a re-branding exercise with a new brandmark that stylises the optical workings of the human eye.

The play of light and tactile feedback is functional beyond mere aesthetics: If you can't make out the logo, it's time to have your eyes checked.

Seeing beyond convention, they designed the boutique's EyeBag in the form of takeaway lunch bags to convey the message that spectacles are as essential as our daily meals.

The boutique's new address is set in big type to literally "grab as many eyeballs as possible" and ensure visibility from a distance.

UTS: THE FUTURE OF FASHION

DESIGN: ZÉ STUDIO
BACKSTAGE/MODELS: CARINE THÉVENAU
RUNWAY: STEPHEN REINHARDT
CATALOGUE/INVITATIONS/WRISTBANDS: ROBIN HEARFIELD

The Fashion & Textiles Program at the University of Technology, Sydney has a reputation of being one of Australia's most innovative fashion degree courses. The Future of Fashion has been developed to further distinguish the program and allow students a new platform for opportunity both locally & internationally. The identity imbues a transcendent style based on a distinct diagonal axis present throughout various collateral such as invitations, a large format catalogue & the runway show. The framework for the identity has been set up to ensure flexibility in content, imagery & art-direction in ensuring the identity of the graduating students each year.

acknowledgements

we would like to thank a
provided & helped our
their learning.

a special thanks goes to t
on the fashion & textile p
& dedication

head of school
lawrence wallen

design academics
armando chant
alana clifton-cunningham
cecilia heffer
vicki karaminas
todd robinson
donna sgro

technical staff
philip inwood
milena ratkovic

school administrat
julian nicholls
anita marosszeky

contact
cecilia heffer
director of p
faculty of d
university o
e: cecilia.h
w: fashion

the future of fashion

gemma anasta *u. destructed bloom.

destructed bloom explores the relation-
ship between fashion & the natural world.
with inspiration drawn from readings of
sustainable design practice. from this
research, the fabrics used throughout the
collection have been embedded with plant
matter as a way of creating colour & texture as well as producing clothing, which
in time, will naturally change itself.

photographer teegan pack. model annaliese
griffth-jones. makeup emma petre. hair
alana hoyle.

g.m.a88@hotmail.com

7

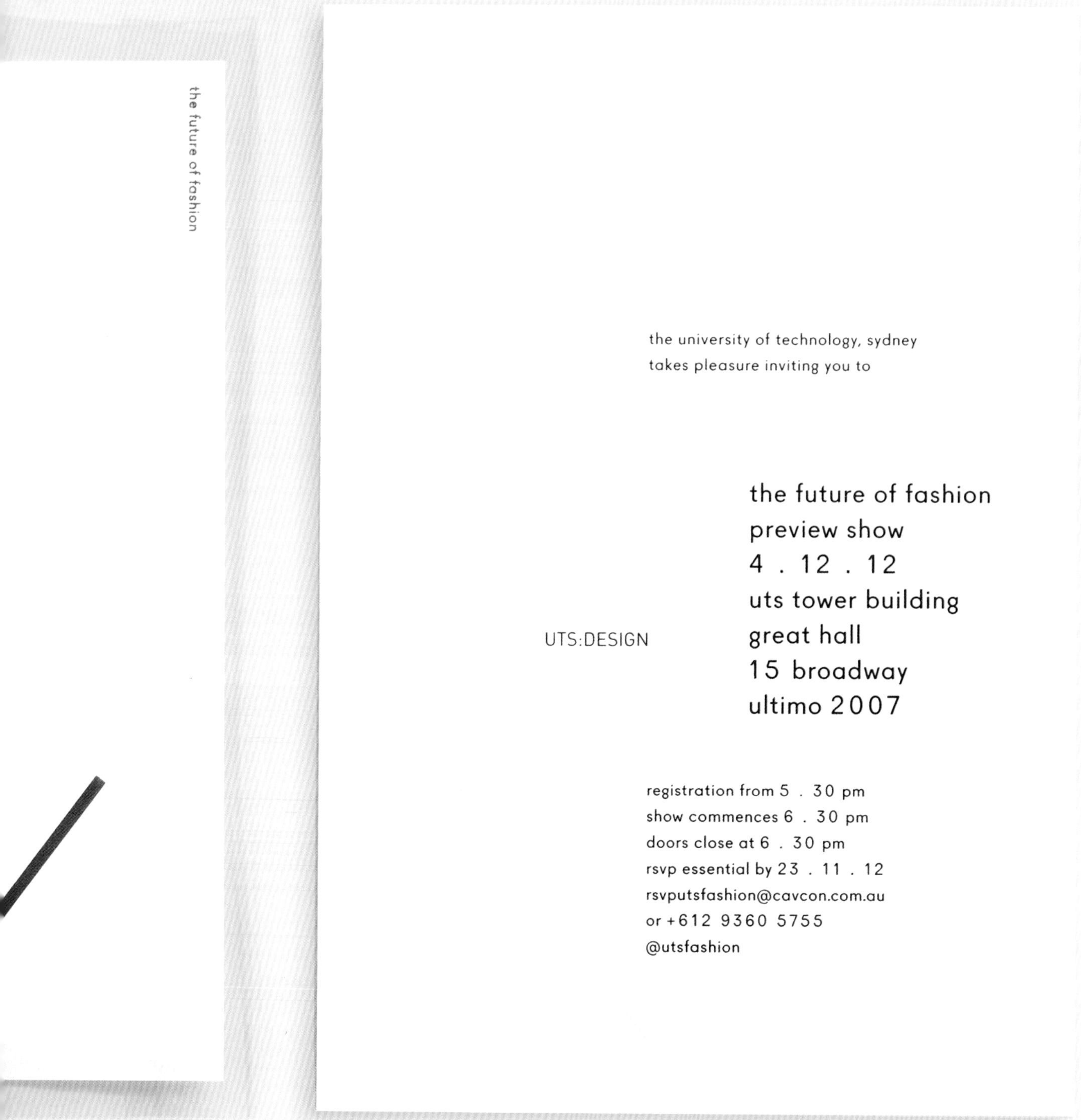

the future of fashion

the university of technology, sydney
takes pleasure inviting you to

the future of fashion
preview show
4 . 12 . 12
uts tower building
UTS:DESIGN   great hall
15 broadway
ultimo 2007

registration from 5 . 30 pm
show commences 6 . 30 pm
doors close at 6 . 30 pm
rsvp essential by 23 . 11 . 12
rsvputsfashion@cavcon.com.au
or +612 9360 5755
@utsfashion

@utsfashion

#futureoffashion

#futureoffashion

fashion

fashion

28127

#futureoffashion

28004

fashion

@utsfashion

Critically acclaimed fashion
designer Lui Hon approached
Latitude to develop a new and
sophisticated direction for his
2011 Autumn/Winter Campaign.
The project developed to
encompass all aspects of the
brand, from the identity to the
collateral production, resulting
in the correct representation of
the Lui Hon vision. Latitude
has worked closely with Lui
Hon & photographer Peter Ryle
on all the following seasons,
and successfully translated the
thoughtful qualities synonymous
with the brand into a digital
experience and online shop.

LUI HON

UI HON

233

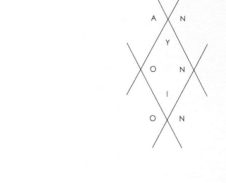

ANYONION – Stick Design Berlin is a fashion label from Berlin, with focus on knitwear
– all styles produced in Berlin in small series. The signet refers to a certain pattern. For the
shooting Raum Mannheim produced the logo in 3-d.

INDEX

has earned the trust from many major corporations and institutions in Hong Kong.

—
Colin Pinegar
colinpinegar.com

Colin Pinegar was born and raised in the mountains of Salt Lake City, UT. He received his BFA in Graphic Design from Brigham Young University in 2011. He currently lives with his wife in the hills of San Francisco, CA.

—
Dalston
dalston.se

Dalston provide creative direction, art direction, branding and design for commercial and editorial clients within the lifestyle, fashion, retail, culture and arts world.

Dalston want to "challenge, simplify and surprise".

Dalston love a challenge and work in all forms of media. Among their projects you can find a selection of art direction for fashion, interiors and entertainment brands, visual communication for packaging, magazines, brand identities, digital applications and exhibitions.

Within their established network of creatives they can tailor complete and unique workgroups for most projects and client needs. This helps them be flexible, and gives each and every project a unique outcome.

—
Daryl Feril
www.darylferil.com

Daryl Feril is a Philippine-based illustrator and designer. Having grown up traveling from city to city, he was able to discover and meet different people from various cultures and environment which in the latter part contributed into his creative work. After graduating in 2012 with a bachelor's degree, he took the freelance plunge with a few background in print and layout.

He was then noticed with his self-initiated personal project "Brands in Full Bloom" that features his new-found personal style of flaura theme, rough hand-drawn sketches, flowing lines & curves and blowing watercolors with the final product composed and polished digitally. He's influenced with ancient designs, nature and fashion which are mostly visible in his works.

He enjoys listening to Jazz/Soul, Country and Indie music which helps in keeping his ideas and inspirations rolling.

—
Designbolaget
www.designbolaget.dk

Designbolaget is a Copenhagen based design studio working at the intersections of art, fashion and culture. They strongly believe in conceptual thinking and original ideas to design bespoke solutions for every assignment, regardless of the actual project scale. A constant dialogue with their clients is as essential to them as the physical act of designing. They focus mostly on printed matter, with great attention to detail and tactile finishing.

Designbolaget was founded in 2002 by Claus Due and has been recognized with numerous international awards.

—
DEUTSCHE & JAPANER
www.deutscheundjapaner.com

DEUTSCHE & JAPANER studio was initiated in 2009 and offers expertise in various disciplines, such as graphic design, product design, interior design, illustration and scenography as well as conceptual creation and strategic brand escort.

The studio focuses on communication, regardless of its physical condition, environmental, haptical or visual, but always in regard of sustainable experiences.

—
Emma Wickström
April.wickstrom@gmail.com

Former Fashion Director for H&M labels, Monki & Weekday. Today Living in LA. Freelancing in photo production and styling.

—
Eps51
www.eps51.com

Eps51 is an internationally active design studio covering a wide range of projects including print, web, brand identity, illustration and photography.

Eps51 have worked on numerous intercultural projects over the past years, mostly for clients from the cultural field.

—
Fabio Ongarato Design
www.fabioongaratodesign.com.au

Founded in 1992 by partners Fabio Ongarato and Ronnen Goren, based in Melbourne, Fabio Ongarato Design is renowned for the diversity of its work. The studio works across a variety of fields such as fashion, corporate, arts and architecture deliberately crossing the boundaries between them.

—
Folch Studio
folchstudio.com

Folch Studio is a Barcelona-based design office founded by Albert Folch in 2004. The studio works across several media: from magazine, poster, visual identity, book and stationery to signage, website, video and exhibition design.

The studio's approach is defined by its engagement with all stages of any given editorial project – from inception to final form, participating actively in aspects that further art direction and merge with edition.

In 2011, the studio started its own publishing venture: The Flames.

—
Founded
wearefounded.com

Founded is a graphic design studio producing creative responses for a varied and international client base. Their work is multifaceted. They create thoughtful, well crafted design for printed and digital use, develop brands and get excited about environmental graphics and product design.

—
Foundry
www.foundrystudio.com

Foundry is a creative agency providing branding, design and direction. They work across a range of disciplines, including photography, illustration, print and digital design, copywriting and other specialisms.

—
Glamcult Studio
glamcultstudio.com

Glamcult Studio is a creative agency based in Amsterdam, the Netherlands. It also publishes Glamcult Independent Style Paper, a fashion, art and music orientated lifestyle magazine.

—
Happycentro
www.happycentro.it

Happycentro was born in 1998 in Verona, Italy. In recent years they have worked with both big clients and tiny startups, for local agencies and major international companies.

Their approach to design is always the same: designing a logo, an advertising page, a wall or directing a commercial offers the same opportunity to deal with a "problem to solve".

Beside commissioned works, they spend plenty of energy in research and testing.

Their formula is: Beauty = (Order/Complexity)•Sweat^2.

Their human diversities are their first resource that expresses itself in never-ending cross links of different inputs, skills, passions and styles.

They don't like doing same thing twice, and prefer going further what they're already able to do. It is tiring but satisfying.

Stop Motion Animation, Tv/web commercials, Packaging, Visual art, Typography, Graphic design, Illustration, Music Videos and Labels are what they do.

—
Helen Marchant & Laura Woolner
www.helenjennifermarchant.com
laurawoolner.tumblr.com

Helen Marchant is a graphic designer based in London. Laura Woolner is a fashion trend forecaster based in London.

—
HORT
www.hort.org.uk

HORT began its inhabitance back in 1994, under the previous stage name of EIKES GRAFISCHER HORT. Eike is the creator of HORT. HORT - a direct translation of the studio's mission. A creative playground. A place where 'work and play' can be said in the same sentence. An unconventional working environment. Once a household name in the music industry. Now, a multi-disciplinary creative hub. Not just a studio space, but an institution devoted to making ideas come to life. A place to learn, a place to grow, and a place that is still growing. Not a client execution tool. HORT has been known to draw inspiration from things other than design.

—
Inklab
www.inklab.com.au

Inklab is an independent design and digital strategy studio based in Canberra, Australia. They believe in working in collaboration with their clients to deliver quality creative. Their diverse team of designers, artists and thinkers, considers each project with fresh perspective to create something extraordinary based on their clients' unique and particular needs.

—
Ironflag
www.ironflag.net

Ironflag is a Copenhagen based design studio comprising of Mikkel Møller Andersen, Kasper Fjederholt and Marco Pedrollo. From both the digital and more tactile end of the creative spectrum, they aspire to utilize their different visual backgrounds to create singular works within the fields of Art Direction and Graphic Design.

—
Jana Jelovac
www.me-livingroom.com

Jana Jelovac was born in Belgrade (Serbia) in November, 1979. She'd graduated in Interior Design at the University of Applied Arts. She is good at various forms of digital arts, graphic design and illustration. She loves sun, animals and sea.

—
Joe Joiner
www.joejoiner.com

Joe Joiner is a Design Creative based in London. His practice ranges across a variety of clientele, media and approach to which he strongly believes in individually tailored, concept-led realisations that portray a sense of playfulness through simplistic execution. Joe works as part of a creative team as well as an individual, seeing projects through from ideas to production.

—
Johan Hjerpe
www.johanhjerpe.com

Johan Hjerpe is a designer based in Stockholm, Sweden. For the past decade Johan has been designing graphics, spaces and strategic frameworks for a vast array of contexts. From working with Sweden as a nation brand, to doing commissions for magazines, artists and fashion designers, stopping over in finance, electronics, white goods, performing arts and more. His work has over the years gained a focus on the sociocultural aspects on people interacting. Design becomes a tool, prop or interface for situations where mutual value-in-context emerge.

—
Johanna Bonnevier
www.johannabonnevier.com

Johanna Bonnevier is a Swedish art director, graphic designer and illustrator based in East London. She mainly works on projects based around architecture, culture and fashion, ranging from both small- and large-scale print jobs to film credits and installations.

—
Joseph Veazey
www.josephveazey.com

Joseph Veazey is a designer and illustrator currently based out of Brooklyn, NY. His work has been featured in CMYK Magazine, Print Regional Design Annual, and American Illustration.

—
Karera
www.karerano.com

Karera is a graphic design and illustration studio in Tokyo, Japan.

—
Kila Cheung
www.kilacheung.com

Kila Cheung graduated from The Hong Kong Polytechnic University. He is now a professional illustrator, graphic designer and one of the founders of "3Pyramid" and a committee member of the Hong Kong Society of Illustrators. Kila values childishness, curiosity, the courage to break rules and dreams.

—
kissmiklos
kissmiklos.com

kissmiklos is a designer and visual artist. Currently architecture, design and graphic design are his workfields. There is an outstanding aesthetic quality and strong artistic approach characterizing his implementation of work. His fine artworks define his work just as the individual perceptioned corporate identity designs and graphics (listed) under his name.

—
Latitude Group
www.latitudegroup.com.au

Latitude is a brand, digital and communications agency driven to create change and deliver results. The team work with businesses, organisations and individuals to harness the true power of their brand and engage ideas that move them forward. They look to align brands with business goals, values, aspirations and market direction to deliver meaningful results.

—
Les Graphiquants
www.les-graphiquants.fr

Les Graphiquants is a design studio based in Paris. Their graphic signature is characterized by highly stylized letterforms, by words that are cut in such a way as to emphasize their etymology, and by clean and well-tempered compositions. They like to draw, refine, and express the more graphic qualities of words. They tend to favor solutions that allow them to steer clear of visual clichés.

—
Luca Fattore
www.lucafattore.com

Luca Fattore was born in Venice in 1990. He had graduated from Iuav University of Venice in 2012.

During his studies he worked as an intern at Studio Tapiro under the direction of Gianluigi Pescolderung and Enrico Camplani. He also worked at Polystudio under the direction of Francesco Messina.

He has undertaken many workshops with important personalities like Jonas Roth and Rasmus Batch of Kesselskramer, Ginette Caron and Cristina Chiappini.

One of his contests in collaborations with his schoolmate Fabio Furlanis, figured in the top forty selected posters of Posterheroes 2nd edition. His projects are featured on Aiap (Aiapzine), Trend List, Inspirimgrafik, Vis-va and other blog of sector.

—
Lucia Freire
www.behance.net/dry

Lucia Freire is a graphic designer specialized in identity and branding from Spain. Among others, she has worked for clients such as Coca-Cola, Fanta, Levi's and Tecel.

—
Manuel Dall'Olio
www.manueldallolio.com

Manuel Dall'Olio is a graphic designer. Since 1994 he'd started to work with communication agencies, companies, artists and publishers and he developed a multidisciplinary attitude and approach to design. In 2001 he founded Trelink Intermedia network with designers from the world of communication, design, fashion and photography. Manuel teaches art direction and graphic design in Accademia di Belle Arti di Bologna. He's Member of AIAP and Icograda.

—
Mark Niemeijer
www.youmaan.com

YOUMAAN is the pseudonym of Mark Niemeijer, a twenty-one year old graphic design student and independent graphic designer from the Netherlands.

Since he was a child, he had been interested in art and eventually this affection led him to graphic design. What moves him in visual communication and plays the leading in carrying out design is to help people express themselves and impress others.

—
Marta Puchala
www.cargocollective.com/martapuchala

Marta Puchala is a London-based creative specialising in art direction, brand identity and illustration. She is a graduate from London Collage of Communication. She is particularly interested in design process, conceptual thinking and problem solving.

—
Natsuko Pursell
natsukopursell.com

Natsuko Pursell is a creative and designer whose work focuses on fashion design, identity, branding, and print. She has collaborated with studios such as iDL Worldwide, Wieden+Kennedy, and NORTH, and has created work for Sephora, Nike, Jordan Brand, and Mira Kaddoura, among other clients. She lives and works in Portland, Oregon.

—
NIGN Company Limited
www.nign.co.jp

Kenichiro Ohara is art director and graphic designer in NIGN Company Limited.
Kenichiro Ohara was born in Hyogo in 1973. After graduating from an industrial high school, Kenichiro has self-taught the discipline of design throughout a wide range of his professional careers. In 2000, he became a freelance designer and in 2006, he founded his own design firm, NIGN. NIGN has been a gateway to an extensive field of design services, including CI, branding, book design, fashion, and packaging. Kenichiro is member of Tokyo Type Directors Club and Japan Graphic Designers Association.

—
Orka Collective
orkacollective.com

Orka Collective is a project of two graphic designers and artists, Abo and Ooli. Orka means "energy" in Icelandic and also it sounds like the name of orca the whale. Orka Collective specializes in graphic and web design and illustration.

—
Raum Mannheim
raum-mannheim.com

Raum Mannheim conceptualize and create the visual presence of their clients and setting them on the scene with graphics, texts, illustrations, installations and photography. The team love the challenge of understanding complex subjects, of giving them structure and precisely implementing them through different media forms. They think holistically; for them, quality lies in detail.

It is not the size of the project that makes the difference, but rather the project-specific tasks and the individual form it takes on - starting from an unusual idea on to a coherent concept and through to a unique aesthetic expression.

Through their own artwork, projects and exhibitions, they are constantly expanding their creative spectrum.

—
Rikako Nagashima
rikako-nagashima.com

Rikako Nagashima was born in Ibaraki Prefecture, Japan in 1980. Graduated from Visual Communicate Design major in Musashino Art University back in 2003, and began to work at AD agency HAKUHODO in the same year. Now she is Creative Director at HAKUHODO. She was awarded by Tokyo ADC Awards, JAGDA New Designer Awards, NY ADC Special Awards and etc.

—
RoAndCo
roandcostudio.com

RoAndCo is a multi-disciplinary design studio devoted to holistic branding that serves a range of fashion, art, and lifestyle clients. Led by award-winning Creative Director Roanne Adams, RoAndCo offers design, image, and branding capabilities across a variety of mediums, from print to moving image. By thoughtfully distilling a client's inspirations, ideas, and motivations, RoAndCo generates fresh, sincere, compelling brand messages that engage and resonate.

—
Samuel Mensah
www.behance.net/smbstudios

Samuel Mensah is a visual artist and designer living and working in London. The young artist and founder of SMBStudios has been working professionally now for 5 years in the industry and specializes in a range of styles from digital art to branding, typography and illustration.

—
Scandinavian DesignLab
www.scandinaviandesignlab.com

Scandinavian DesignLab is an independent design agency based in Copenhagen, Denmark with representation in Shanghai, China.

Identity – is their core business with the vision of building corporate souls, which actually identify and distinguish, and envisioning product brands that connect with the target, build preference and win the battle at the moment of truth.

—
Shang-lun Yang
shang-lun.com

Graduated from Pratt Institute/ Communication Design, Shang-lun Yang

combined his strong interest in fashion with his passion toward graphic design. He tries to blend in fashion elements into different project whether it's branding, interactive, motion or editorial design.

—
so+ba
so-ba.cc

Susanna Baer and Alex Sonderegger were born in Switzerland. They started their design studio "so+ba" in Tokyo in 2001. With their experiences in graphic design and advertising in Switzerland and Japan, as well as a good understanding of the two very different cultures, cross-cultural communication is one of the strength and the focus of so+ba. so+ba is active in the field of graphic design, art direction, and teaching typography and design.

—
Somewhere Else
www.somewhere-else.info

Somewhere Else is anywhere other than here & now.

They are about the constant shift away from the ordinary; the persistent journey to create work that goes beyond the basic need to communicate.

Through their design and conceptual processes, they provide distilled solutions that translate strategy into visuals inextricably adding value to businesses. Together with their broad range of clients, the team continually pushes to create unique works that are idea-driven, relevant, long lasting and intelligently crafted.

Be it through branding, art direction, way-finding systems or anything in between, Somewhere Else strives to create works that can inspire, humor or even touch the audience.

—
Studio Newwork
www.studionewwork.com

Studio Newwork is a graphic design studio based in New York. They assemble a team of passionate typographic designers with commitment to search for excellence in design.

—
StudioSmall
studiosmall.com

StudioSmall was established in 2004 by founding partners David Hitner and Guy Marshall. They provide creative and strategic art direction and design for advertising, branding, packaging and online.

The team are experienced across fashion, lifestyle and hospitality sectors worldwide.

—
StudioThomson
www.studiothomson.com

StudioThomson are a multi-disciplinary creative agency specialising in design & art direction formed in 2004 by brothers Christopher and Mark Thomson.

Their approach to every project is from a unique perspective. They collaborate with the best creative talent available and their love of research, craft, and innovative creative concepts produces work that is classic and contemporary with a very British twist, earning them a global reputation.

They like to do great work and have fun doing it, forging long term client relationships whilst providing consistent, clear, intelligent solutions that communicate with impact.

—
Studio SP-GD
www.sp-gd.com

Studio SP-GD is the design studio of Surya Prasetya. They specialise in graphic design which includes but is not limited to; printed matter, identity & branding, exhibitions, fashion, websites etc.

—
The Drop
thedropstudio.com

The Drop is a creative studio devoted to making ideas happen through the execution of innovative concepts, brands and designs.

Founded by brothers Nick Thomm & Josh Thomm, The Drop has quickly established itself as a young forward thinking studio, with an impressive client list of major international brands; including MTV, Red Bull, Nike, L'Oreal and the BBC.

The Drop is focused on pioneering a truly in-house studio approach, successfully working across identity, graphic design, web development and the art, film and photography industries.

—
Two Times Elliott
www.2xelliott.com

Two Times Elliott is a design consultancy based in Notting Hill, London. Two Times Elliott produces a diverse range of work across multiple disciplines including print design, identity and web. They help their clients communicate their message clearly and intelligently.

They deliver intelligent bespoke design solutions and advice to a wide range of clients, from individuals to large organisations, in a variety of different sectors.

Two Times Elliott like to work with all their clients as creative partners and to this end they think it is important to involve their clients in the design process as much as possible. They also work hard to manage their design work intelligently alongside a client's budget.

The team is made up of passionate and experienced designers all of whom are experts in a variety of disciplines. They are also passionate about giving new young design talent studio experience where they can work with the team to boost the vigour of their projects and generally augment the creative process.

—
Viktor Matic
www.viktormatic.com

Viktor Matic is a multidisciplinary designer and creative all rounder in a wide range of cultural sectors. Viktor describes his current work as the "post-internet design practice", which is seeking a way out of common everyday patterns and notions. He believes that interesting things nowadays appear in border areas such as art and design, music and fashion, culture and science, media and activism. At the same time Viktor is equally interested in implementing the best solutions for both visual-aesthetical territory, and on the conceptual and ideological level. Viktor Matic is creative director and co-founder of the artists and music collectives "WupWup" & "Tanzen ist auch Sport".

—
VTWOB
www.vtwob.com

VTWOB is an art direction studio and a wondrous think-tank created to fulfill the requests of its most pressing clients.

The studio team is specialized in various segments of art direction, from brand development to editorial design, and from packaging to advertising, not to forget event management, interior design and the web universe.

Since recently, it also provides a service of digital pr so as to unleash the full communication potential of its clients.

—
Ward Heirwegh
www.wardheirwegh.com

Ward Heirwegh (1982) graduated in 2007 as a master in typography at the Sint Lucas academy in Ghent, Belgium. In 2009 he started his independent practice as a graphic designer and art director, mailing expressing an interest in editorial design. Next to his studio he also founded a research-based, ephemeral platform for artist publications called Sleeperhold Publications. So far SHP has released a photobook, a silkscreen posterset, a deck of gaming cards, a collection of short stories and several vinyl records. Next to these outputs Ward is also giving lectures about his design and research work.

—
Zé Studio
ze-studio.com

Zé Studio is a Sydney based studio that creates valuable design experiences & delivers unique solutions to clients. Remaining true to design that is informed and well considered — their design leaves no excess.

Zé Studio was initiated by Joe Tarzia in early 2011 & began as an exploration of well communicated design. With a passion for the arts and culture, the team strives to grow their involvement in this sector, and continue to work on identities & brands of any scale.

ACKNOWLEDGEMENTS

We would like to acknowledge our gratitude to the artists and designers for their generous contributions of images, ideas and concepts. We are very grateful to many other people whose names do not appear on the credits but who provided assistance and support. Thanks also go to people who have worked hard on the book and put ungrudging efforts into it. Without you all, the creation and ongoing development of this book would not have been possible. Thank you for sharing your innovation and creativity with all our readers.